Praise for ICONIX

"In this age of accelerating complexity, it is a pleasure to be introduced to Wolfgang's beautifully illustrated book—to just settle back, smile, and be reminded of the forgotten, simple objects that we live with and enjoyed in the past, present, and future."

—Charles W. Pelly, former president of
the Industrial Designers Society of America
and founder of BMW-Designworks

"An amazing time travel machine! This inventory of the iconic objects of our daily life is a reference for all of us, but also for our design schools and their students."

—Maurille Larivière, cofounder and president
of The Sustainable Design School, Nice, France

"This collection is a timely reminder that not everything has been digitally transformed. Talented human beings, designers who care passionately about the people who will use their designs, continue to inspire. Form-making that will become iconic the way these are is not easy; but worth learning how. This is an exceptional guide in the quest."

—RitaSue Siegel, founder and partner,
RitaSue Siegel Resources

"*Iconix*, what a perfect name for Wolfgang's new book!! Amazing how he has illustrated the everyday products we use that have become the symbol and representative image in our minds for a whole category of products, e.g., Carousel Projector, Apple MacIntosh, Walkman. Design is global."

—Dana Wolcott, adjunct professor
and lead innovation coach at
Rochester Institute of Technology

ICONIX

Exceptional Product Design

Wolfgang Joensson

Skyhorse Publishing

Skyhorse Publishing books may be purchased in bulk at special discounts for sales promotion, corporate gifts, fund-raising, or educational purposes. Special editions can also be created to specifications. For details, contact the Special Sales Department, Skyhorse Publishing, 307 West 36th Street, 11th Floor, New York, NY 10018 or info@skyhorsepublishing.com.

Skyhorse® and Skyhorse Publishing® are registered trademarks of Skyhorse Publishing, Inc.®, a Delaware corporation.

Visit our website at www.skyhorsepublishing.com.

10 9 8 7 6 5 4 3 2 1

Library of Congress Cataloging-in-Publication Data is available on file.

Cover design by Wolfgang Joensson

Print ISBN: 978-1-5107-3039-7
Ebook ISBN: 978-1-5107-3040-3

Printed in China

Contents

Acknowledgments

"It takes a village to write a book" was the exasperated advice from my sister-in-law, Dr. Cindy Ott, a fine author and professor of American history. Her entertaining, yet instructive writing style has been a leading example for me. She is right to point out the necessity for help from others, which is why I would like to thank her and the following people for their support and help.

First in line is Ian Ferris, a brilliant designer who came up with the idea that I should write and encouraged me on my way. Several of my designer friends have motivated and helped me choose the icons: Tim Toomey, Dieter Wanke, and Ronald Ihrig. My business partner, Lutz Gebhardt, discussed with me and also contributed icon ideas. His unwavering support and enthusiasm is just one of those life forces everyone should have around.

Having designed but never written before, I relied heavily on the patient support, editing, criticism, and overall inspiration of my muse and partner in life, Susan Kuntz. Her relentless will to drop everything and discuss my book was highly appreciated throughout the process. From the very early pages on, she has diligently worked with me on the content and made sure the result is presentable. Without her, this book—and my life— would not be half as good.

The wonderful Anne-Laure Guiard-Schmidt has not only boosted my confidence in myself from the first day I met her and during the making of this book, but was also instrumental in finding the title. Jim Peterson and Jonathan Duff, both great writers, have helped me to understand writing better, and I thank them for their time and effort. John Flint, a former editor, has helped me tremendously by suggesting reading material to improve my writing and advising me on how to make my text better. He has also painstakingly edited everything.

As a designer, I want to create all visuals by myself, but I am smart enough to know when to ask for help there, too. Urs Stemmler, a great transportation designer, helped me with ideas and criticism regarding some icons. Angelika Scholz, as often in my past, once again gave me advice on typography. The architect Jon Schultz has enthusiastically helped from the start with tasteful advice to improve contents and design.

My gratitude also goes to my editor, Nicole Frail of Skyhorse Publishing, who has diligently edited my writing, researched for verification, and corrected mistakes I made. You helped a great deal to make this book perfect.

Last but not least, a big thank-you to my brilliant agent, Fran Black from Literary Counsel, who is the best agent any writer could have: supportive, highly professional, perfectly organized, and a lovely person.

This is the village of my friends, and I consider myself lucky to have them.

Design Creates Memories

Do you remember the first product you bought for yourself? That Sony Walkman for listening to your favorite music? Or the Swiss Army knife you got as a present from your uncle? Can you recall your mother making cake with the KitchenAid mixer? Such products keep us company from the cradle on. Some even find their way into our memories—and our hearts.

This book is about personal relationships with objects, but it is also about the impact designed objects can have on us as a society. Every one of them contains meaning: cultural, historic, social, or emotional. For example, when several German mineral sources get together and decide to have a unified bottle to be more visible on the market, this becomes important for public health, since their product competes with less healthy sugar-based soft-drink choices. To have a common package design makes their product more visible next to international sweet-drink giants.

What makes a product iconic is a common response based on individual feelings. Without emotions, there are no icons. Although emotions are personal, when many people react in the same way, their judgment provides a common ground for evaluation.

I use the term iconic in a different way from linguists or semiologists. A strictly scientific

approach to design is insufficient, for designers also care about emotions, and that can rarely be done in a systematic or predictable way. Nor can their approach be called purely artistic, for they also care about function, production, and how the product will find its way into the hands of a customer. It is this duality that makes design such an exciting activity. Blending function and form demands an understanding of emotions as well as logic and science.

Every serious designer aims to create objects that endure the test of time, become coveted and influential. Iconic products are even more valuable— if not directly, then by the value they add to the brand they represent. SONY, for example, has never been more fashionable than during the high time of the Walkman, a product coveted by everyone, but particularly youngsters.

Since I started to work as a designer, I have been interested in what makes design appealing, noteworthy, and, most of all, memorable. There are many good ideas and pretty shapes, but it takes more to make an icon. It is fascinating to see how the designers on the following pages shaped our surroundings and improved our lives through the creation of innovative objects of beauty and desire.

What Makes Products Iconic?

Iconic products are memorable, and to be memorable, they have to stand out and be different. More than that: they have to be better than the rest. What makes products superior and anchors them in our minds is either an innovation or a content to which we can emotionally respond. With these two components, a product can become an icon—a representative of a category, of an era, or of a spirit.

Havaianas are the ubiquitous sandals. These flip-flops have come to stand for beach life—and not only in Brazil. They evoke summer, care-free times, minimalism, and basic comfort.

Only quintessential products give you the feeling you are seeing not just a lamp, for example, but *the* lamp—if not the top-quality one, then perhaps the one with the most advanced technology, or the one that makes you do a double take and think, *This one is special*. You feel it.

This is an emotional response to a successful communication between the designer and you. When it is shared by many people, the product has attained "iconicity."

How does that happen? There are two main avenues: to imbue the product with emotional content, or to stimulate by innovation. Emotional content can be based on function, while innovation tickles our curiosity and arouses desire.

Understanding the user is the key to any design solution. After a new product has been produced and marketed, it has to be sold, but most important, it will be used. This is where human expectations come in. Before we consider a purchase, we look at the object. We try to read it. We expect hints about function, but we are also open to an emotional appeal. We like to like.

As users, we want stuff that works and that we understand. We also want to enjoy the products we buy as long as possible. In other words, we want practical, intelligible, quality products.

Intelligible design helps us see how something works. We appreciate a sophisticated product, but we must be able to understand it. We want to know where the top and the bottom is and how to open, refill, or maintain it. We users need clues. A remote control is useless if we cannot change the batteries when they are dead.

We want quality. But without consumer feedback or expert advice, we have to rely on whether the product looks solid. The real factors that influence sturdiness—the type of material, wall thickness, and construction—are not usually obvious. Expression of quality becomes as important as quality itself.

Aside from making users feel good about a product by matching their expectations regarding its reliability and longevity and assuring them that they do not need to read an instruction manual, what can be done to delight their senses? Understanding of provenance and respect for the environment, if communicated well, incite a positive emotional reaction with everyone. With provenance, I refer to where the product was build, and by whom. The country of origin and the brand that represents the circumstances of production is something we associate with values—something we can relate to. Respect for the environment does not only include sustainability, which people have come to expect; it also means the environment where the product will be sold—we shop differently online from in a boutique, a supermarket, or a high-end department store. And we feel differently about those choices. Every product exists also in a historical context, and if we see the time we live in reflected by the design, then this makes us feel good. And whenever we feel good, chances are greater that we remember it.

New things attract us, but so do familiar ones. Market research shows that user groups tend to prefer the well known, so for new designs, acceptance is always an uphill battle. That means that designers shouldn't copy existing solutions, but create designs that provide orientation by using proportions, shapes, or details we know. Successful design provides visual clues about the product, but it avoids borrowing an identity from something that already exists.

How to make something new? More important: how to make something better? Innovation is the solution—to apply an existing principle to a new area. Whereas invention makes new use of the laws of physics, innovation is invention's little sibling and easier to plan. A designer can have three new ideas by next Thursday about how to dispense coffee into a cup. Coming up with new ways to make coffee instead is not that easy. For its manageability, its appeal to people, and its power to impress, innovation is paramount.

Innovation exists on various levels. An alarm clock with a glass cover for travel is a neat little innovative idea. Sometimes the main function is innovative. When the product starts a new category, like a smartphone, then the entire product is innovative. Innovation can also be visual—and should be. Great ideas have to be discernible. When you add a corkscrew to a pocket knife, show it. Then it will be understood and will sell—the prerequisite for becoming useful and adopted.

Form should communicate function. If one is new, the other has to be, too. In most iconic products, however, form and function are both innovative, for function is not only technical: a toaster not only browns bread but is also part of the morning ritual, the home decor, and maybe a celebration when gifted.

There are no appearances without significance or connotation, and our perception of forms is influenced by everything we have seen before. New or familiar, every form means something. It is the designer's responsibility to ensure that the form he chooses expresses the meaning he wants to convey. Form is much more than "just a shape"—in the words of the French writer Victor Hugo, it is contents rising to the surface. There is always a relationship between what something is and what you see. Form is anything but superficial: it is profound. At least, to be iconic, it has to be.

Communication through form between designers and users of an object is neither obvious nor self-evident. Our emotional responses as users to visual stimuli are individual and, of course, subjective. Design is not science. We cannot measure design, but that makes it only more exciting and challenging. The most important phenomenon in life escapes such quantification— emotions. And though you cannot calculate them, they count. Emotions are the reason why there are no fail-safe paths to make people understand a design. This makes the examples in this book so impressive: these designers managed somehow to leave a note understood by many. Remembered over time, that is what made them iconic.

ICONIX

How to make a curvaceous sculpture from a tree? Cut it into strips, lathe them, then bend those over steam around a form. The result is ingenious and an example of beauty and practicality. Unassembled, three dozen chairs fit into a single box. To allow spilled liquids to drain quickly, woven cane material was used for the seat. This made it perfect for Austrian coffee houses, hence its nickname Wiener Kaffeehausstuhl. At a time of mostly one-off furniture, this one was notable for its serial production process. No other product better marks the beginning of industrial design.

THONET
Chair No. 14
Austria 1859
Michael Thonet (German-Austrian)

To contain fizzy liquid without losing pressure, you need a tight seal. In this bottle, a glass marble pushed up by the pressure of the carbonation does the trick. The red rubber ring and the glass intuitively express that function. To pop the top, you merely had to push down the marble with your thumb. Only problem was kids loved to smash the bottle and play with the marble.

HOPE GLASS WORKS
Mineral Water Bottle
United Kingdom 1873
Hiram Codd (English)

A bottle with dimples makes it easier to grasp when pouring a dram or two. This functional advantage also gave character and a strong image to this elegant form, so much so that the brand of whiskey sold in the bottle adopted Dimple as its own name. It is distinctive also as being the first bottle shape to be patented in the United States.

DIMPLE
Bottle
Scotland 1890
unknown

Fold it away. That's what you can do to reduce the risk of cutting yourself with an open knife blade. Add a corkscrew to open that bottle of wine, and you have a very practical and extremely versatile tool. A limitless variety of models has been launched, but the basic idea remains—a useful, handy, and quality utensil right there in your pocket.

Wester & Co.
Pocket Knife
Germany 1890
unknown

A pleasing ergonomic handle, sculpted from wood, a simple twist-lock, *et voilà!*—a tool so emblematic of French culture that it has become the generic name for any wooden-handled knife. Unchanged for more than a century, this vital utensil is found not only in many households, but also in workshops of craftsmen and artists. Even Pablo Picasso sculpted with it, proving that perfection can be truly inspiring.

OPINEL
No. 10 Knife
France 1897
Joseph Opinel (French)

The brush feels soft in the hand, and its smooth curves make it easy to grasp. The flexible red-rubber cushion holds the bristles—an innovation labeled "pneumatic" by the creator. Almost unchanged from the original design and still available well over a century later, this is proof that no better brush has ever been conceived. The shape's simplicity is striking, giving it a timeless elegance.

MASON PEARSON
Hairbrush
United Kingdom 1885
Mason Pearson (English)

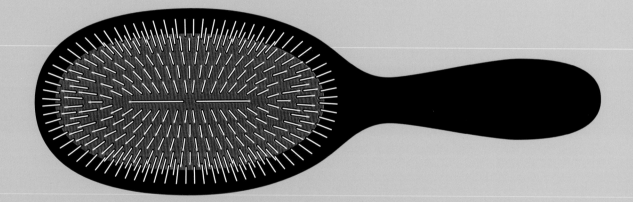

With its combination of feminine curves and phallic profile, this is probably the most recognizable shape in the world. It is also the first bottle ever to be patented. With a form that evolved over many iterations, it always kept the characteristic emblematic shape, embodying a sensuality that made it distinctive.

Coca-Cola
Bottle
United States of America 1915
Earl R. Dean (American)

Almost a century old and nearly unchanged, this product combines a robustness with a design that evokes familiarity and conviviality. You see where the motor sits. The stand swings protectively around the bowl. Easy to understand, ready to mix, it blends ingredients, but it also blends into the kitchen environment.

KITCHENAID
Mixer
United States of America 1918
Herbert Johnson (American)

Although the first telephone booth was erected in Berlin in 1881, it is the British version that has become more evocative. Its design draws on visual imagery from architectural artifacts like tombs and galleries in London. With a dome-shaped roof, intricate paned window structure, and bright-red color, the booth has become synonymous with the British capital and English culture. Even if you've never been to London, you've surely seen them in the movies.

K 2
Phone Booth
United Kingdom 1920
Giles Gilbert Scott (English)

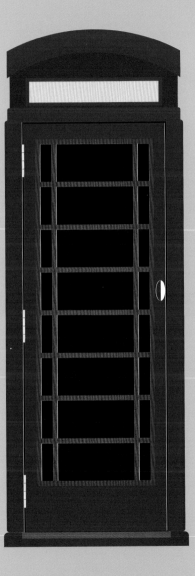

The glass sphere gives a warm glow—that's comfortable. Light is directed to the desk it stands on—that's practical. The choice of glass and chrome—that's modern. This lamp represents the Bauhaus design style (basic geometric forms, material honesty, and serial production) in an exemplary way. Its purity is striking, even today.

Table Lamp
Germany 1924
Wilhelm Wagenfeld (German)

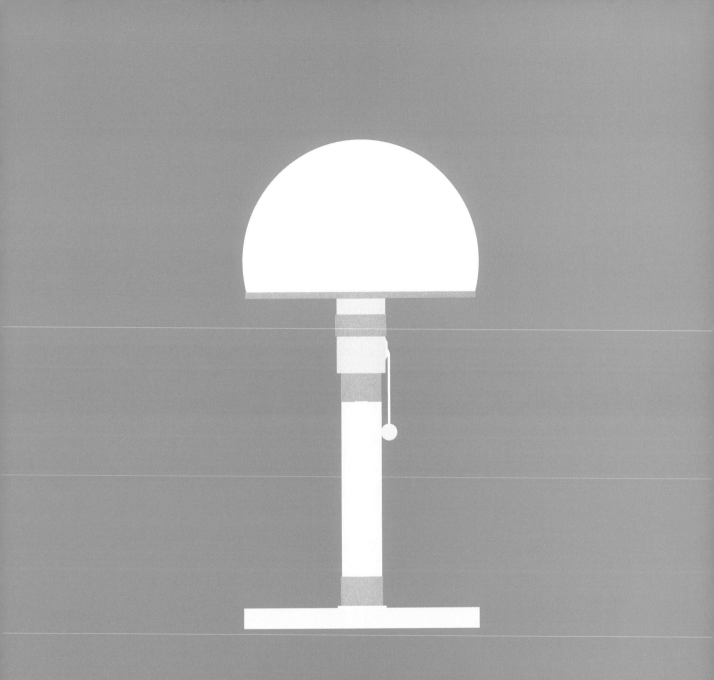

French love their food and their women, so it should not be surprising that they charmingly refer to this casserole as a *cocotte*: an endearing word for women in general but also for *une belle-de-nuit*, a girl-of-the-night. Available in multiple colors, its production is solidly hand-finished and its design almost unchanged since its inception. Many unforgettable meals, lovingly prepared and served in it, have certainly contributed to its iconic status.

LE CREUSET
Dutch Oven
France 1925
Octave Aubecq (French), Armand Desaegher (French)

The time must have been ripe. Three designers—Mart Stam, Le Corbusier, and this one—had similar ideas almost simultaneously of how to improve seating comfort. All three capitalized on the metal tube's flexibility and resiliency to create a chair that rocks slightly. It feels softer than the material suggests, bouncier than typical four-legged chairs. This model was not the first but became the most successful, probably because the combination of industrial steel with traditional woven cane makes it versatile for office as well as dining, and it looks sleek even today.

THONET
CANTILEVER Chair
Germany 1928
Marcel Breuer (Hungarian)

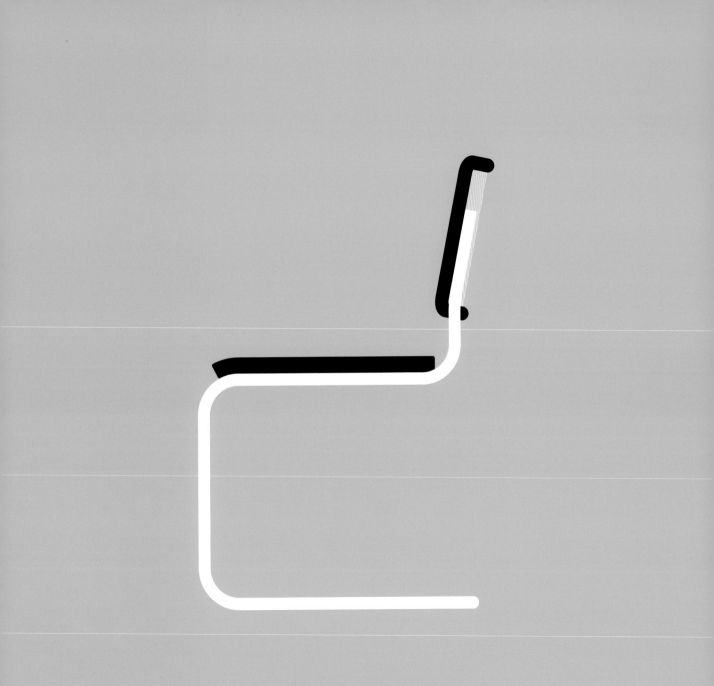

The future never seemed closer nor more desirable than in the early thirties of the last century. Coming out of the Great Depression, people embraced technology with a romantic fervor. Everything had to be aerodynamic. The winds of change certainly influenced the shape of this product. The creator, an industrial design pioneer, created a practical item here, which was also an excellent representative of an era focused on style.

Iron
United States of America ~1930
Walter Dorwin Teague (American)

What you see is what you get. With a visible and adjustable infusion, true tea lovers can prepare their brew exactly as they like. All it takes is removing the glass sieve filled with tea leaves in time. The design's rigorous restriction to one material speaks of purity yet is soft and evocative in its shape. Total transparency is achieved with elegance and panache.

SCHOTT
Tea Pot
Germany 1931
Wilhelm Wagenfeld (German)

You want a highly adjustable desk lamp that remains in position once fixed in place? This auto mechanic used his knowledge of car shock absorbers to create a product that is functional, practical, and comfortable to adjust. He and his business partner also created the name. The lamp has so much character and personality that an animation company chose it for its company logo.

Anglepoise Lamp
United Kingdom 1932
George Carwardine (English)

Disseminate propaganda! This was the secret objective that brought this radio into people's homes. A deceptively simple loudspeaker box, it communicated its purpose unwittingly. The blend of Bakelite with a woven loudspeaker cover and the rounded edges softened its appearance in an attempt to integrate it into the home. Successful and insidious.

DR.G.SEIBT
VE 301 W "Volksempfänger" ("People's Receiver")
Germany 1933
Walter Maria Kersting (German)

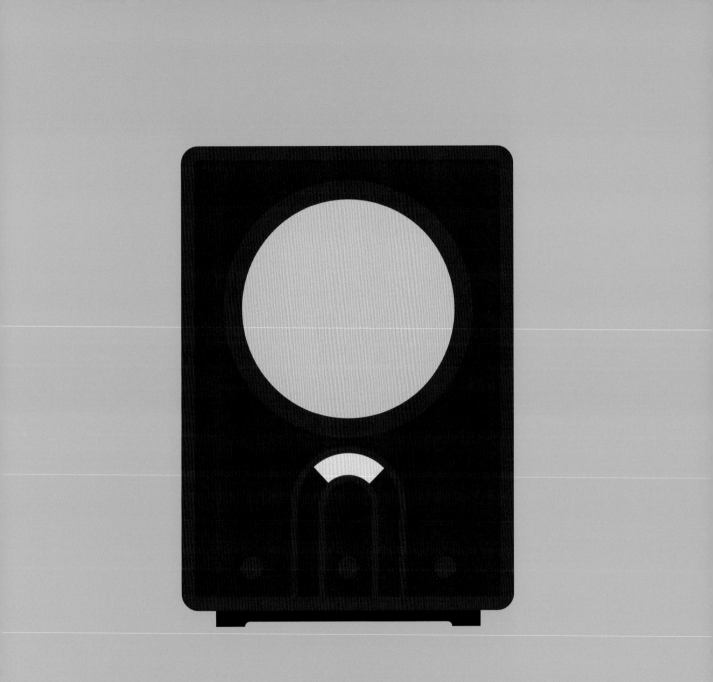

Whatever the weather, this baby will light your fire. A great invention that made our lives simpler and more comfortable, just as the zipper that inspired its name. This solid product works reliably in any conceivable adverse condition. Launched just before World War II, it won a place in the pockets and hearts of countless military and civilians. Thanks to its serviceability and strong build, it is still on the market today.

ZIPPO
Lighter
United States of America 1933
George G. Blaisdell (American)

To highlight the colors and quality of the glaze, this company's design director used stepped concentric circles. With this quintessential product of the Art Déco period, you could set a festive table with a variety of pieces in a range of colors. During World War II, the product line was disrupted because the source of the red-color version was uranium, which caused concern about radiation as well as its need for the war effort. The manufacturer then lost faith in the product and discontinued production for more than a decade. The whole line was relaunched in 1985 and is seeing a strong revival today as a retro design.

LAUGHLIN CHINA CO.
Fiestaware
United States of America 1936
Frederick Hurten Rhead (English)

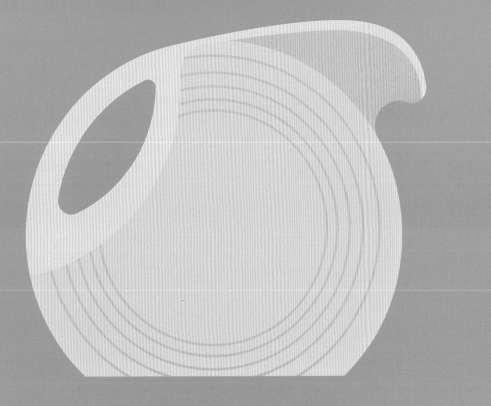

Nowadays, we talk into devices that look like flat bricks, but in the early days, in order to determine the perfect ergonomic angle between the mouth- and earpieces of telephones, this design office measured hundreds of people's heads. With those measurements, they created the first phone-to-house ringer and network circuitry, based on an Ericsson model created by the Norwegian artist Jean Heiberg. By the standard of those days, it provided good acoustic quality. Collectors lovingly refer to it as the Lucy phone, a common prop from *I Love Lucy*, the popular 1950s sitcom.

WESTERN ELECTRIC
302 Phone
United States of America 1936
Henry Dreyfuss (American)

"You push the button, we do the rest!" This manufacturer's slogan was targeted at people who liked photography to be simple. The name of this model, featuring a smooth body in pure Art Déco design, emphasized lightweight construction and sturdiness. Raised lines provided just the right grip on the otherwise smooth metal surface. Nothing distracted from the focus on easy operation, which proved the slogan to be true.

KODAK
Bantam Special
United States of America 1937
Walter Dorwin Teague (American)

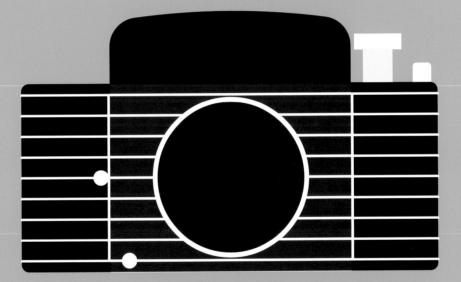

Thumb-sized, this camera was still tightly packed with sixty patented inventions by the engineers. The result was practical and easy to use, particularly for covert operations against an enemy. Originally a precision instrument with new camera technology made entirely from metal, it lost its luxury appeal over time. With an increasing amount of plastic parts and the low-resolution images provided by its tiny negatives, it could not compete with better-performing modern devices. That was the end of this model.

MINOX
Riga Camera
Latvia 1936
Walter Zapp (Latvian)

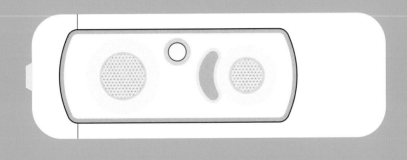

When fire destroyed the stock of this Cologne luggage manufacturer—all except the aluminum raw stock—the owners turned disaster into success. The result was a lightweight suitcase fashioned from this metal. With sturdy outside ridges, which gave it high stability, it evoked the progressive aviation age. The company continued to innovate and in 2000 introduced the first suitcase with two polycarbonate shells zipped together, still with the same identifiable ridges to maintain its strong brand image.

RIMOWA
Aluminum Luggage
Germany 1937
Richard Morszeck (German)

The original patent for Morgan Parker's two-piece scalpel dates to 1915. When it expired, this British manufacturer refined and perfected the tool. The simple ergonomic shape and surface pattern convey its function. That unmistakable and distinctive image has become synonymous with its use in surgery as well as for arts and crafts. With this product, its manufacturer became the world leader it still is today.

SWANN-MORTON
Scalpel
United Kingdom 1937
unknown

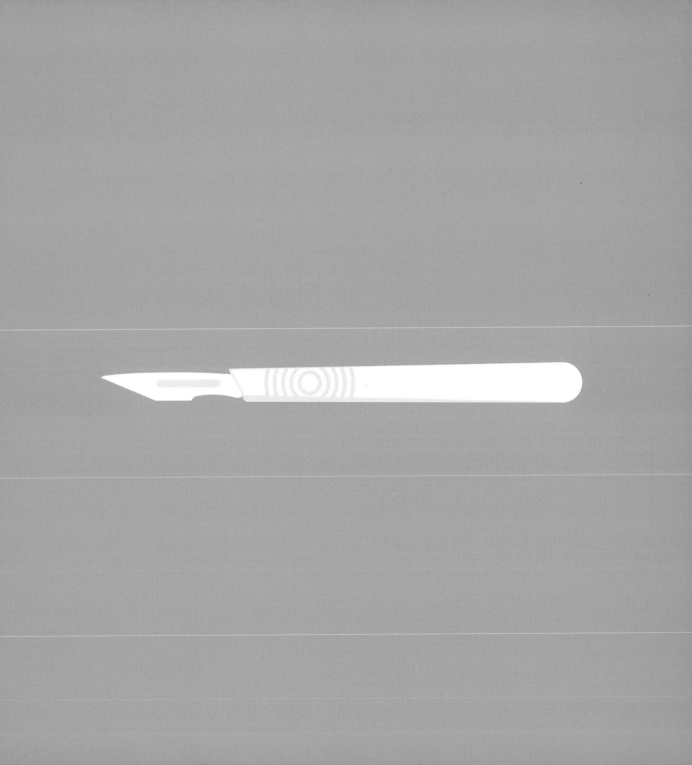

Spare, yet very expressive, the strict form of this espresso maker renders the process intuitive. When you fill it with water and heat it on a stovetop, the water will boil and expand. This pushes the hot water upward, through the sieve with the coffee grounds in the middle of the device. Steam pressure then forces the espresso to rise to the top. The company's owner recognized the iconic status of his famous product, requesting that his remains to be stored in one for his funeral ceremony.

BIALETTI
Moka Express
Italy 1933
Alfonso Bialetti (Italian)

This founder's son traveled to America during the 1929 Wall Street crash. Sensing an opportunity, he decided to produce luxury lighters, catering to clients not affected by the crash. The first ones were produced in aluminum, since the more resilient brass was a strategic material restricted to war purposes. The lighter became known for its outstanding quality. For some time in the sixties, all lighters from this company were made of eighteen-karat gold, with a small percentage of brass. Sleek lines and geometric decorative patterns made it one of the most socially acceptable men's jewelry pieces of the time.

S.T.DUPONT
Lighter
France 1941
unknown

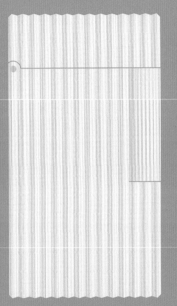

A box with a hole pretty much describes the original brownie camera in 1900. It took a little more time to become the emblematic product named after the Brownie cartoon character created by Palmer Cox. Easy enough for children to use and robust enough for soldiers to take into battle, it became a line of simply constructed and inexpensive cameras. Suddenly anyone could become a photographer. Artistic people saw the camera's potential, and together with some of the photos taken with it, the camera itself became iconic.

KODAK
Brownie Six-20
United States of America 1946
unknown

Every clock shows the time. This one not only displays the actual hour and minute, but it also shows the time of its genesis—the postwar (WWII) era. It reflects people's desire to have fun again. With numerals playfully replaced by brightly colored spheres, this instrument magically changes from a device that conveys precision and reliability to one engendering a lively mood with hope for a more promising and brighter future.

HOWARD MILLER
Ball Clock
United States of America 1947
George Nelson (American)

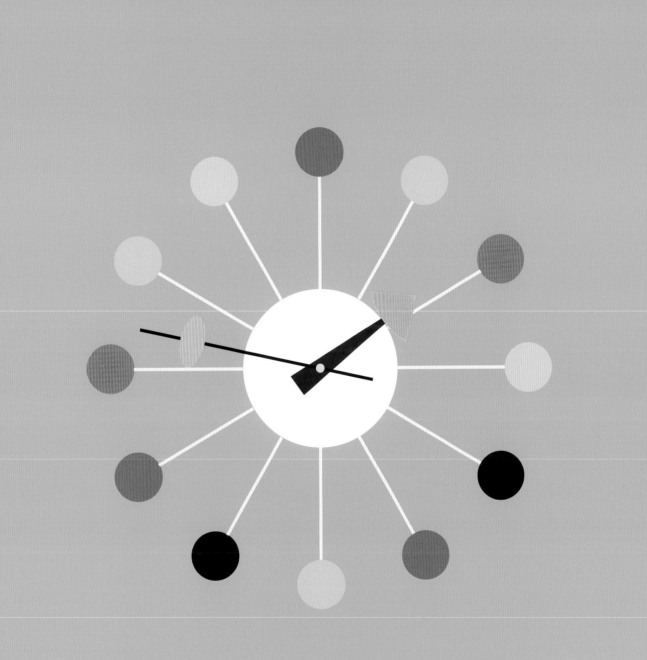

"The only truly original and beautiful design for such an object"—so said the photographer Edward Steichen. Minimalism personified, it needs only two hands and an orientation (here provided by a slightly concave polished twelve o'clock disk) to show you the time. An impressive reduction, a testament to the creator's talent.

MOVADO
Museum Watch
Switzerland 1947
Nathan George Horwitt (American)

Early cathode tubes for television sets were round. The image displayed on them was square. The challenge: to find a good compromise between those extremes. This one met that challenge with a beautifully sculpted form, reminiscent of Art Déco architecture. Emphasis on ventilation slots provides an architectural look like a power station, while the dark-colored casing draws attention to the screen.

BUSH
TV 22
United Kingdom 1948
unknown

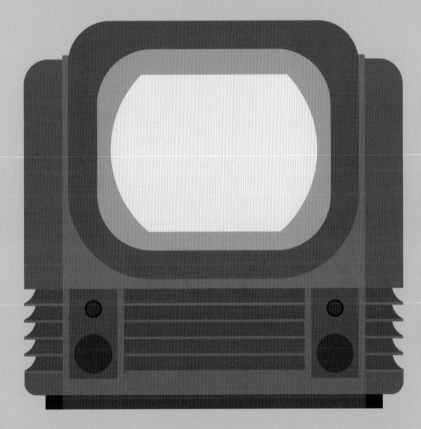

How does one transport a basket filled with raw eggs on a bumpy country road without breaking them? The creative briefing was a challenge, but the car's innovative suspension met it with élan. With unsurpassed practicality and a shape that raises emotive responses, it is arguably the car that most deserves to be included in a lineup of iconic products. Its value-retention is amazing, too. Originally developed to make farmers more mobile, it has since been driven by generations of people, with or without eggs.

CITROËN
2CV
France 1948
Flaminio Bertoni (Italian)

Fountain pens blot. Newspaper ink is more viscous and dries faster than regular ink. In 1938, László Bíró turned this observation into a pen with patented ball mechanism and sufficiently viscous ink. Marcel Bich (the company name is a simplified version of his) and his partner Edouard Bouffard bought the patent. They developed this pen, which today is the world's best seller with more than 100 billion sold. With its simple, ergonomic shape, it does not roll off the table and is known for affordable quality.

BIC
Cristal Pen
France 1950
Décolletage Plastique (French)

For Italians, when making coffee, the result is what counts.
The preparation can become a ceremony. Resembling a
miniature factory, this machine promises and produces
rich espresso with low caffeine content. Its high-quality
appearance is due mostly to the polished chrome surface,
which announces: expect the best!

PAVONI
Europiccola
Italy 1950
unknown

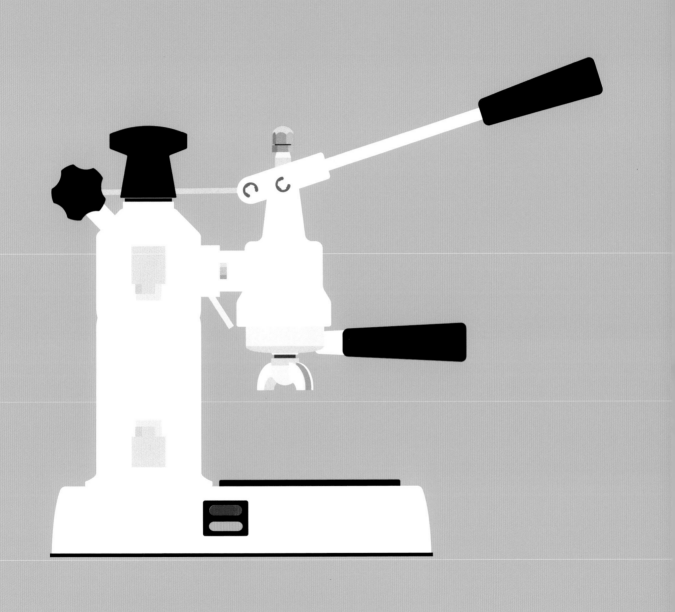

Nothing speaks more of summer and backyard barbecues than this archetype of grills. An inspired worker in a marine buoy factory turned the two parts of a buoy into the prototype of today's well-known product. Refined continuously over the years, its rounded shape efficiently contains heat and is easy to clean. A sturdy wheel base makes it mobile for use in the yard or garden.

WEBER
Grill
United States of America 1950
George A. Stephen (American)

You want to be a star? Not so easy—but looking like one is. Don these shades and you're halfway there. Comfortable to wear, the shape—neither too rounded nor too edgy—is easily recognizable. Ubiquitous use by movie stars has made the black-rimmed lenses with the small almond-shaped detail synonymous with fame.

BAUSCH & LOMB
Ray-Ban Wayfarer
United States of America 1952
Raymond Stegeman (American)

This "magic stick" (English translation of Zauberstab) turns you into a culinary wizard in no time. So perfect was the original construction that only few small changes have been made since its launch. The recognizable ergonomic silhouette of this reliable device has won a place in the kitchens of professionals and passionate amateurs alike.

ESGE
Zauberstab
Switzerland 1954
Acton Bjørn (Danish)

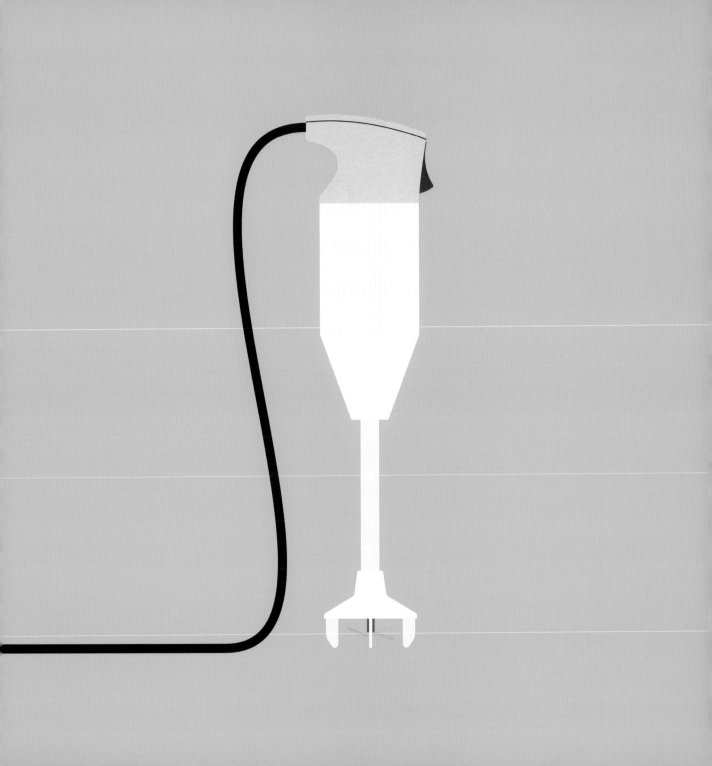

Good enough for Eric Clapton and Buddy Holly. With a two-tone, contoured shape and three pickups (a first) for richer sound quality, it was created to enable people to play and enjoy music better. Many instruments evoke an era or a musician, but this one merits a mention on anyone's short list. The fame of many great players has rubbed off on it.

FENDER
Stratocaster
United States of America 1954
L. Fender, B. Carson, G. Fullerton, F. Tavares (all Americans)

Close your eyes and think of England! If you see a red double-decker bus, then you may have the same steadfast appreciation for tradition as the Brits. To go from Oxford Circle to Piccadilly, all you had to do is hop on the rear platform. Its characteristic vertical outline makes it one of the most recognizable city vehicles in the world.

LONDON TRANSPORT
Routemaster
United Kingdom 1954
A.M. Durrant, Colin Curtis, Douglas Scott (all English)

It's so easy to dismiss a bowl as being just a bowl! This product, however, does the job right—enough to become memorable. A little handle and a small spout, and (since the sixties) a rubber foot to reduce slippage. Made of temperature-tolerant thermoset plastic, the hard surface is nearly scratch resistant, unlike cheaper versions in thermoplastic material. It features a rounded inside for easy whisking and vertical walls to save space in the fridge.

ROSTI
Margrethe Mixing Bowl
Denmark 1954
Sigvard Bernadotte (Swedish), Acton Bjørn (Danish)

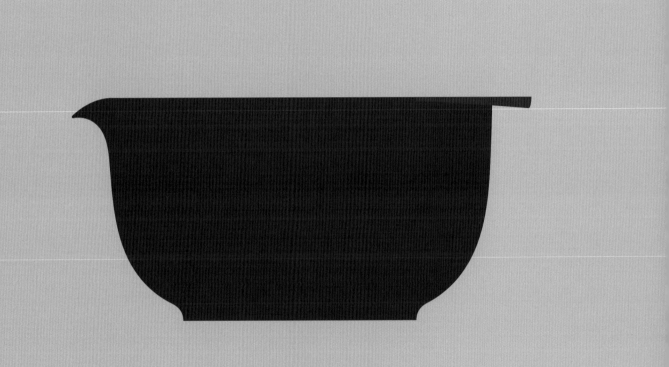

Do you dream of flying through Italy with a partner sitting behind you? You need a motorized two-wheeler to share the joy. There are lots, but this one has made it into the hearts of scooter enthusiasts. Its image is universal, evoking dreams of vacations in the land of *la Dolce Vita*.

PIAGGIO
Vespa
Italy 1946
Corradino d'Ascanio (Italy)

No fairy-tale character is buried in this radio/record player combination despite its nickname of "Snow White's coffin." But this radical departure from the old style of home audio equipment does mark an end of an era. Only the wooden sides are reminiscent of the previous style, where radios looked like furniture. The modern appearance, with bent perforated steel, reflects a change in music taste in postwar Germany to include jazz and rock 'n' roll. The plexiglass cover protects the record player and dials. It's also the reason for the nickname.

BRAUN
SK 4
Germany 1956
Hans Gugelot, Dieter Rams (both German)

No, it's not an iPod, though it does resemble the audio entertainment device launched half a century later. This product was manufactured by one of the most design-oriented companies of its time, a radio manufacturer founded by a mechanical engineer. It set standards in brand image continuity, including graphic design of its instruction manuals, packaging, and product design. No wonder today's designers and brands are still inspired by their early peer's efforts.

BRAUN
T3
Germany 1958
Dieter Rams (German)

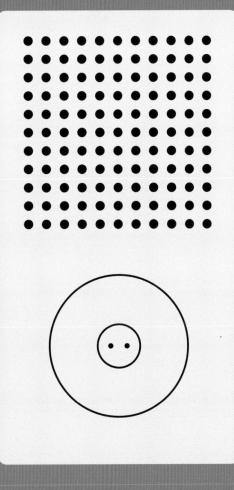

It sounds paradoxical: hide the bulb, but let the light shine through. Curved metal sheets in a sophisticated arrangement make it possible. The overall impression is one of complexity, yet lightness. The creator—an architect—was inspired by a vegetable. He left his mark by designing whimsical lamps like this one.

LOUIS POULSEN
Artichoke Lamp
Denmark 1958
Poul Henningsen (Danish)

You wanted to be in here—at least if it
was the rolling index (hence, rolodex) of
an important person. A Danish engineer
working in New York had the idea of
facilitating access to the addresses of
one's business contacts. The result
was so popular that its name became
generic—a dream of every company and
one of the hallmarks of iconicity.

ROLODEX
Address File
United States of America 1958
Hildaur Neilsen (Danish)

This speaks Bauhaus: no decorative pattern, basic geometric forms. Yet despite their clarity and rigor, the tools never compromise at the expense of the user. Their ergonomic design and dishwasher-friendly stainless steel marked a new age in dining culture. Every modern set of cutlery descends from this bold statement of purism.

MONO
A
Germany 1959
Peter Raacke (German)

TV sets were not always portable. In fact, this was the first. It also had a revolutionary look. Instead of a square box surrounding the tube, the housing continues the tube's shape to the back. The mobility and futuristic style set it apart from the competition. Considered at the time a luxury product, its success was unfortunately compromised by its price, and so it didn't sell well.

SONY
8-301
Japan 1959
unknown

Stackable china is a good idea, taking less cabinet space at home and in restaurants. This robust professional tableware could withstand abuse, which was also an advantage in your kitchen. Its innovative modular system with plates, cups, bowls, jugs, and creamers was originally conceived for public tables, but it was also popular in private households. It's still available today.

THOMAS
TC 100
Germany 1959
Nick Roericht (German)

Accuracy in a watch is rather important. Here for the first time, instead of a balance wheel, a tuning fork keeps the rhythm. This watch shows off its supreme technical innovation right on its face. Visible workings on the front made it notable and heralded its position in the vanguard of timekeeping.

BULOVA
Accutron
United States of America 1960
unknown

Some ideas are so simple. A hole for a broomstick makes it easier to lift the heavy marble base of this lamp. The creators, two architect brothers who preferred common sense and straightforward design, were inspired by streetlights. A two-part lampshade allows light to be directed where needed. It appeared in an iconic James Bond movie, which accelerated its path to fame.

FLOS
Arco
Italy 1960
Achille & Pier Castiglioni (both Italian)

A magic drawing board that can be used forever.
A stylus displaces gray powder on the back of a
screen. One knob moves the stylus horizontally,
the other one vertically. The lines remain—until
you shake the box and the powder coats the
screen anew. Developed by a French technician,
it was named the most popular drawing toy of
the twentieth century.

OHIO ART COMPANY
Etch A Sketch
United States of America 1960
André Cassagnes (French)

A legless chair, elegant, stackable, made from one piece of material. This could only be done with the development of modern plastics. At first, it was manufactured from polyester, reinforced by hand-layered glass fiber—more artisanal than industrial. After considerable investment in molds, it was then produced in polystyrene, which reduced the sales price. To improve the chair's longevity, polyurethane foam was subsequently used. Finally, polypropylene made it even more affordable. All versions spoke to the possibilities of appealing plastic furniture with a flowing organic shape.

VITRA
Panton Chair
Switzerland 1960
Verner Panton (Danish)

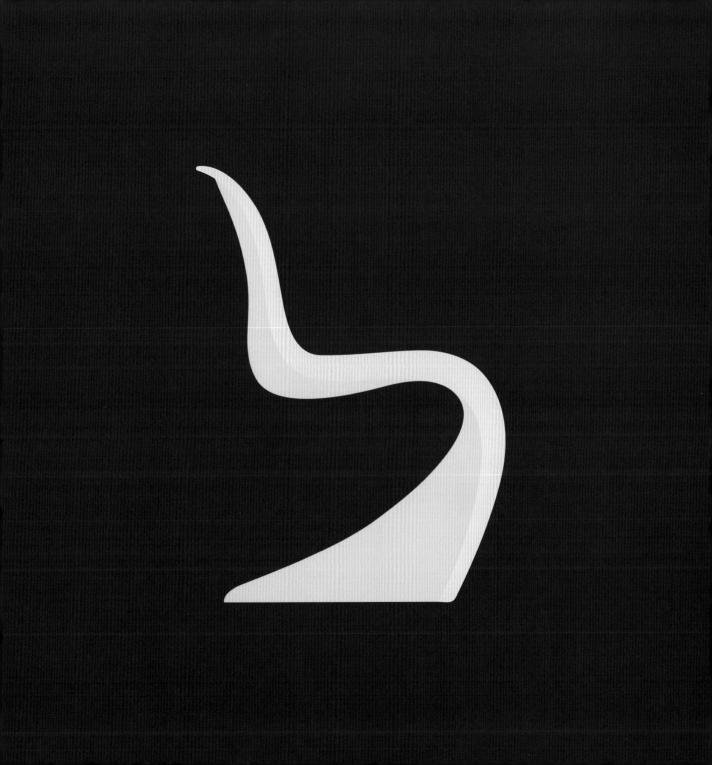

A golf ball that writes. Letters arranged on a small sphere were pushed against the ribbon to mark the paper. By replacing the ball, you could change the fonts. This new technology brought flexibility to typing, a first step toward desktop publishing. The generous futuristic curves of the machine reflected the innovative level of the product and helped inspire those sitting in front, writer's block or not.

IBM
Selectric
United States of America 1961
Eliot Noyes (American)

How to package a key ingredient of Japanese cuisine? This gifted Japanese designer mastered the challenge. He created a modern bottle that expressed the ancient heritage of liquid containers. The simple form pleases. A smart detail—the double spout—lets you pour from either side, and the size of the spout nibs allows you to control how much you want and how fast. The red cap's color evokes traditional oriental lacquer techniques and their predominant color scheme.

KIKKOMAN
Soy Sauce Bottle
Japan 1961
Kenji Ekuan (Japanese)

Blenders have to stand rock solid. This one not only does that, but it also looks the part. The angle of the cone-shaped base facilitated extraction from the mold during production, an important constraint in the early days of plastic household appliances. Its profile speaks of stability, power, and efficiency and has been sold for longer than half a century.

BRAUN
MX 32
Germany 1962
Gerd Alfred Müller, Robert Oberheim (both German)

Shaving your face is supposed to be a manly activity, so these designers created a masculine grooming device with this black razor—previous models were as pale as soap. They also made in-depth ergonomic studies and created multiple wooden models that ultimately led to this shape. When the perforated patented foil head touched the face, beard stubbles passed through the holes and were cut off. Sharp blades never touched the skin, which resulted in a close, smooth, and superior shave.

BRAUN
Sixtant SM 31
Germany 1962
Hans Gugelot, Gerd A. Müller (both German)

To go barefoot in summer is fun, but risky—your feet may need protection. These sandals provide as close to a barefoot feeling as you can get. They promise relaxation, vacation, and no worries. Originally created for the Brazilian soccer team (hence the national colors) these instantly recognizable shoes say "beach!" in every detail. No longer popular only in South America but worldwide, they are now available in a panoply of colors and patterns. Planned as inexpensive shoes and sold for fifty cents, they can now be found priced for dozens of dollars.

HAVAIANAS
Flip-Flop Sandals
Brazil 1962
Robert Fraser (Scottish)

Who doesn't love 3D images? Since 1839, people have been fascinated by stereoscopy, and this extends to today, when virtual-reality glasses provide the same experience with moving images. This 3D slide-viewer was initially made of Bakelite. After the introduction of lightweight thermoplastic, it became cheaper to manufacture, easier to handle, and gained success worldwide.

VIEW-MASTER
Model G
United States of America 1962
unknown

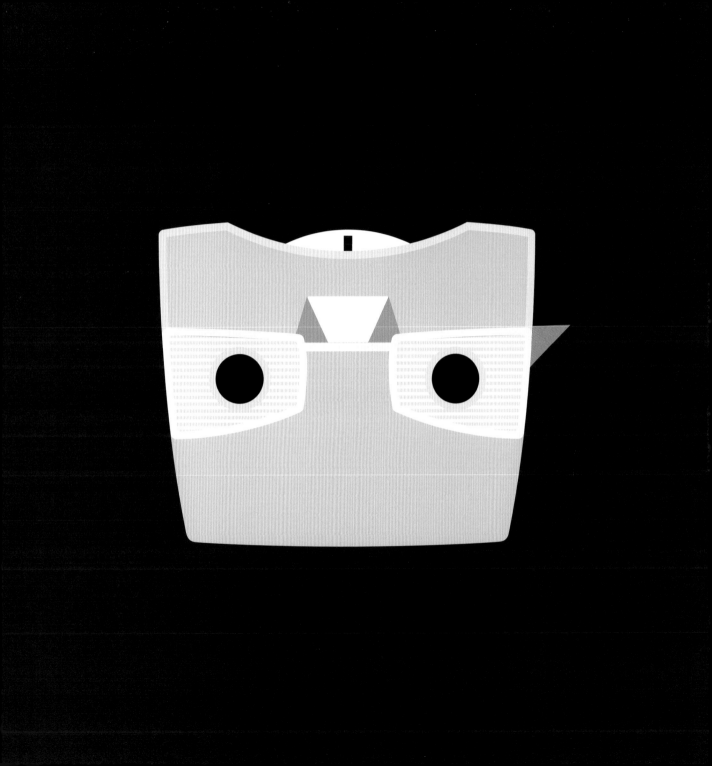

The die is cast. At least it was when these two brilliant designers worked on a portable radio. It consists of two hinged parts. When the colorful shells are opened, they display controls and the loudspeaker. When closed, the carrying handle and the antenna retract, and the resulting shape is round and smooth all over.

BRIONVEGA
Cubo Radio
Italy 1963
Richard Sapper (German), Marco Zanuso (Italian)

Show and tell. From the sixties to the nineties, no presentation by an ad or design agency was conceivable without the use of this slide projector. The magazine contained 80 or 140 slides, which was sufficient to visually explain complex scenarios to an audience. Magazines could easily be switched, and presentations using several carousels could be projected in parallel. This was a forerunner to today's computer multimedia presentation.

KODAK
Carousel
United States of America 1963
Hans Gugelot, Reinhold Hacker (German)

Smudged ink is messy; it stains your sleeve or blotches your document. That dilemma impelled this company's president to invent the felt-tip pen, the first one to use this technology. Liquid ink is directed to the tip through fibrous material, with the benefit that it dries much faster than ink from a fountain pen. With the same design for over half a century, the body has a hexagonal section to prevent it from rolling off the table. Simple and efficient.

PENTEL
Sign Pen
Japan 1963
Yukio Horie (Japanese)

Here's looking up at you! This TV set makes it easy to view even when positioned on the floor. That was important for young college kids or first-time homeowners who might not have had all their furniture yet. The cuddly rounded shape, frameless tube, glossy and brightly colored plastic housing, and quirky antennas all spelled cute and friendly. A flexible and mobile solution for people who moved often.

BRIONVEGA
Algol 11
Italy 1964
Richard Sapper (German), Marco Zanuso (Italian)

Two billion personal computers are in use in the world today. This is their ancestor—the first programmable desktop computer. It did not have a screen. Results were printed on a roll of paper and data memorized internally or on a magnetic card. Marketed as the more familiar "calculator" to overcome fears of potential users, it had neither integrated circuits nor microprocessors, since they were not yet available. Previous computers were as big as wardrobes. The architect who designed this model used the opportunity of a smaller size to create a personal object.

OLIVETTI
Programma 101
Italy 1964
Mario Bellini (Italian)

Making hard materials look soft is the source of this lamp's appeal. Any good desk lamp directs light where needed. This one uses very few parts and is bent in a way that fulfills the task with minimum effort. No extraneous parts just for show—this is decorative minimalism at its best.

O-LUCE
Spider
Italy 1965
Joe Colombo (Italian)

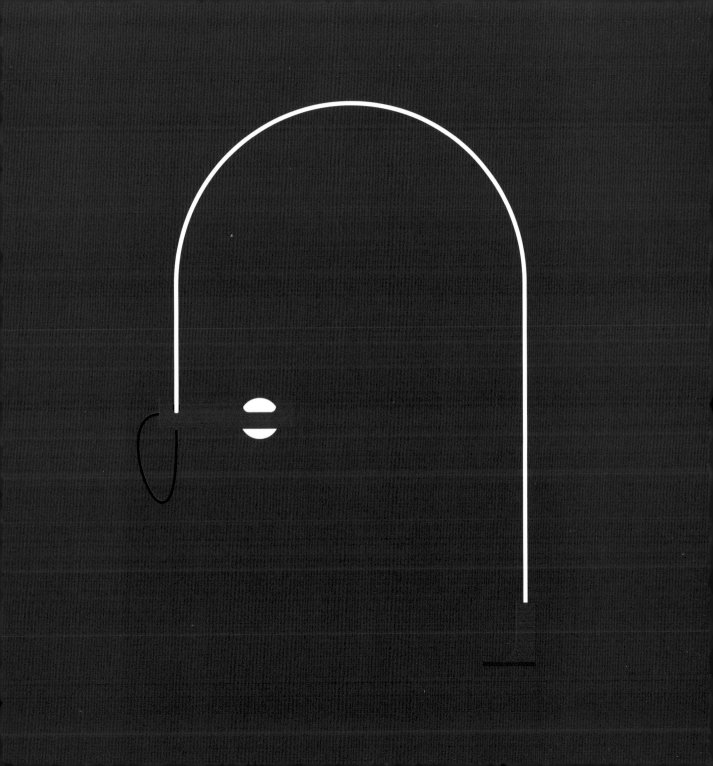

A bulb within a bulb—what a concept for a lamp. This one is truly representative of the Pop Art era. It ironically enlarges the shape of a mundane light bulb and repeats the image inside with a real one, all to create a lamp nonetheless. It is the product of a creative genius who successfully navigates between art and design. Although mass-produced, it can still be considered a piece of art. That alone makes it notable.

STUDIO M
Bulb Lamp
Germany 1966
Ingo Maurer (German)

Where are those scissors? Even if you live alone, you probably misplace yours at times. Orange handles make these easy to spot. They are the best-known product of a company that started as a foundry in 1649 and that produces steel and steel products from axes to steam engines. There's even a left-handed version, as the enhanced ergonomics are dexterity-sensitive.

FISKARS
O-Series
Finland 1967
Olof Bäckström (Finnish)

Good package design reveals what's inside. The little raised bubbles mimic the sparkling water in this bottle. Together with the waist, they also improve the grip. To compete with soft-drink giants, German water sources unified the packaging for their mineral waters with this bottle. Produced by the billions, it's difficult to imagine how this design could be improved.

GDB
Mineral Water Bottle
Germany 1968
Günter Kupetz (German)

We typically take pictures to capture moments. That's why the process should be easy. This company always focused on making photography simple: point and shoot. The model's uncluttered design looks as simple as picture taking should be. A new film format, supplied in cartridges loadable in broad daylight, and a rotating cube with four flash bulbs, made sure it was. This product opened the market even more for consumers who wanted to record visual souvenirs without having to get technical.

KODAK
Instamatic
United States of America 1968
Kenneth Grange (English)

A light switch should be as simple as possible, but not any simpler. You shouldn't have to be Einstein to switch on the light, after all. This designer reduced the form language to the extreme: cable and housing are round, the switch itself square. This nicely emphasizes the importance of the process with a design that remains in the background.

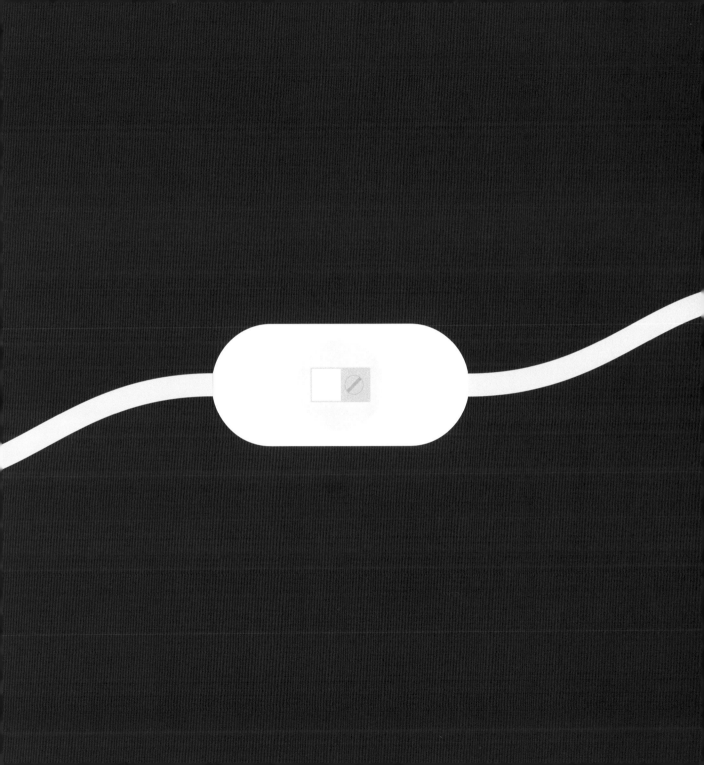

Sometime the best ideas come when you're on the move. This product was advertised as "for all places except the office," and people loved its transportability as much as its round shape and glossy red plastic. It needed the advent of modern plastics to turn the mundane typewriter into a fun tool. Mobility was enhanced by a collapsible grip on the back and a cover from which the typewriter emerged, as if from a drawer.

OLIVETTI
Valentine
Italy 1969
Perry A. King (English), Ettore Sottsass (Italian)

Keep calm and drink tea—and make sure your teapot is as serene as the experience. Here, one material and one color harmoniously unify the elements. Glossy and matte surfaces separate handle and spout from the main corpus. The goal of the Bauhaus founder and architect was to subtly indicate, but not overly emphasize, the different functions of the various parts.

A hairdryer does not have to look like a gun, though early hair dryers often did. They were also bulky and, if made of metal, had safety issues. When this company began to produce a new line of appliances in plastic, it challenged standardized shapes. Dryers typically consisted of a motor, a vertical handle, and a horizontal air outlet. This easy-to-hold model has both air intake and outlet on the front, which results in a smaller package and better portability.

BRAUN
HLD 4
Germany 1970
Dieter Rams (German)

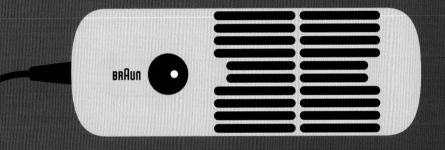

Nobody likes cables. Although electric light was a boon to mankind, we can do without the stringy hassle. Here, low voltage is conducted through the two bars that hold the head, insulated by red plastic elements at the hinges. Instead of springs and complicated mechanisms, the lamp head is balanced with counterweights. It lends an image of serenity to this beautiful object, which is reinforced by its smooth movement.

ARTEMIDE
Tizio
Italy 1972
Richard Sapper (German)

A simple, little, but magical idea—a light box. Closed, it's off. Open, it's on. Clever and puzzling. The light can be directed with the reflective lid. You always wonder: when closed, is it really off? And how does it know?

CINI & NILS
Cuboluce
Italy 1972
Franco Bettonica, Mario Melocchi (both Italian)

One and one is two. But what is 7,568 divided by 0.3492? No need to think with this portable calculator in your hand or pocket. After mechanical, electric, and then electronic ones, this device represented a giant leap in its field and took only a short time to dominate the market. With higher precision than a slide ruler and much easier to use, this early model captivates with the organization of keys, display, and function switches. A protective clear cover clips on the back.

DENNERT & PAPE
Aristo M 65
Germany 1972
unknown

Form interacts with function. This provides the interest and appeal of this lamp. It consists of a bent tube with a weighted steel wire threaded through it. The weight keeps the steel string taut, and because of the bend, there is friction that keeps the tube from sliding down the wire. The lamp, which sits on the tube, can easily be adjusted to any height just by moving it up and down.

FLOS
Parentesi
Italy 1972
Achille Castiglioni, Pio Manzù (both Italian)

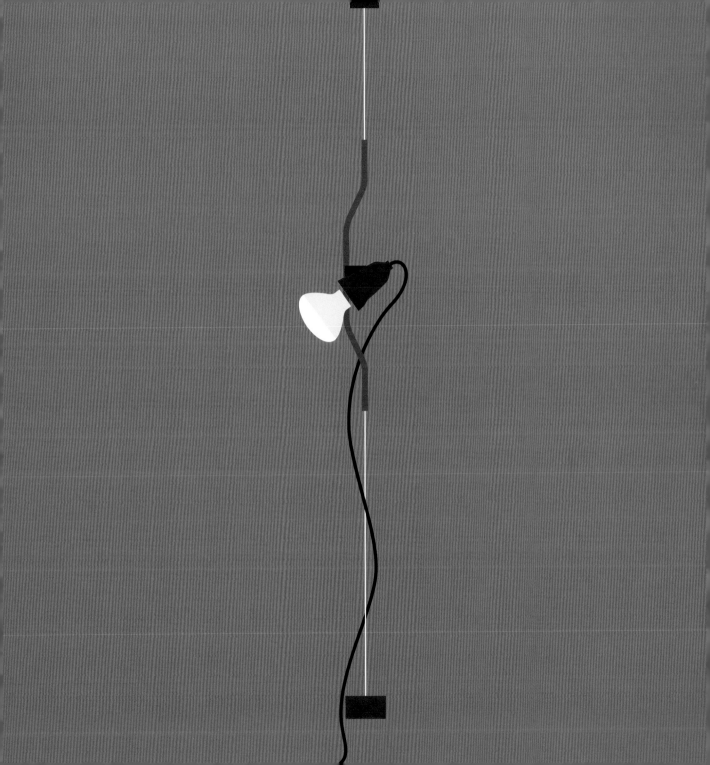

How to protect a portable calculator from potential environmental hazards? By completely encasing it in rubber, including the keys. Even the electronics inside are protected, making them impervious to accidental liquid spills. With a look like no previous calculator, it readily communicates that this is an innovative idea.

OLIVETTI
Divisumma 18
Italy 1972
Mario Bellini (Italian)

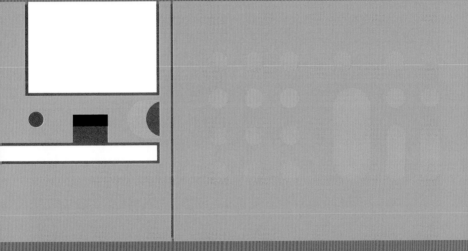

Patience is a virtue. For those who didn't have it, there was Edwin Land. One of the last true inventors of our time, he developed instant photography so we no longer had to wait for the results. Surprised by the success of his first "polaroid" camera—a name alluding to the polarizing filters his system required—he still thought it too bulky. A paperback book size is what he had in mind. The result was this camera and the parallel development of color polaroid film, representing the pinnacle of his career.

POLAROID
SX-70
United States of America 1972
Henry Dreyfuss (American)

There was a time before computers when television was our main electronic contact with the outside world. With a nod to its role at the center of many households, this designer created a sculpture that was appealing from all sides, including the back. Parts made by plastic injection molding encased the working elements. The creators gave users' emotional needs priority over functional constraints and captured this in the catchphrase "form follows emotion."

WEGA
TV 3050
Germany 1972
Esslinger Design (German)

This fits in the fist, and with its soft curves and smooth surfaces, it easily slips into our pockets. It is designed to keep us company. The brand known for its pens decided to branch out into disposable lighters. The result, created by a brilliant and versatile designer, became immediately popular. With a smooth red surface for the push-button valve and a knurled texture for the starter wheel, the indications of functional parts are clear and simple.

BIC
Lighter
France 1973
Louis Lepoix (French)

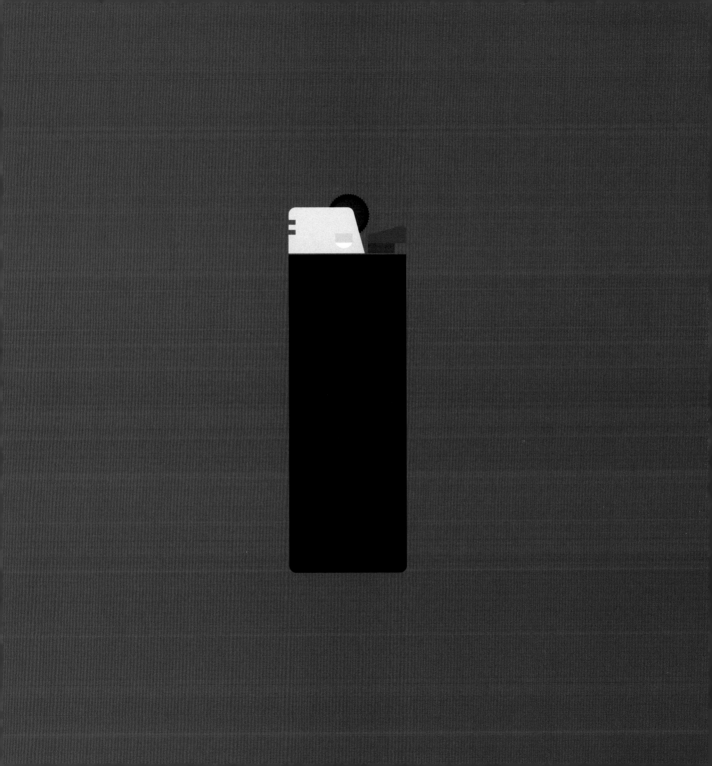

This watch sends signals. The protruding yellow, blue, and red spheres to stop and adjust time show this watch is different. They're also easier to twist. But there is more. The asymmetrical design allows more freedom of movement for the wrist, since the watch rides higher up the arm. Traditional watch materials were abandoned in favor of aluminum and rubber. A high-contrast watch dial completed the new look.

LIP
Dark Master
France 1973
Roger Tallon (French)

One of the early electronic watches, this timepiece was designed for the lower price market in both kit and assembled versions. It provided unparalleled accuracy, even when compared to very expensive mechanical watches. The face featured a clear separation into three horizontal areas. The top one housed the display. The middle one had a button hidden under soft plastic left and right, to show time or count seconds. The bottom gave access to replace batteries from the back. With just a black plastic strap and red LEDs, it had a touch of the mysterious and magical.

SINCLAIR
Black Watch
United Kingdom 1975
Clive Sinclair (English)

What you see is what you get. Clean, simple lines with few parts. The light bulb is half covered by a silver-colored reflector that directs it downward. A cage around it protects the user from touching the hot metal. The fitting has a switch, the cable hangs free, and the hinged steel rods allow for easy angle adjustment. Simple bent steel profiles are easy to produce but provide for a fully functional and adjustable lamp with character. This production method allows for extending the brand to wall-hanging, standing, and desk models.

ARTEMIDE
Sintesi
Italy 1976
Ernesto Gismondi (Italian)

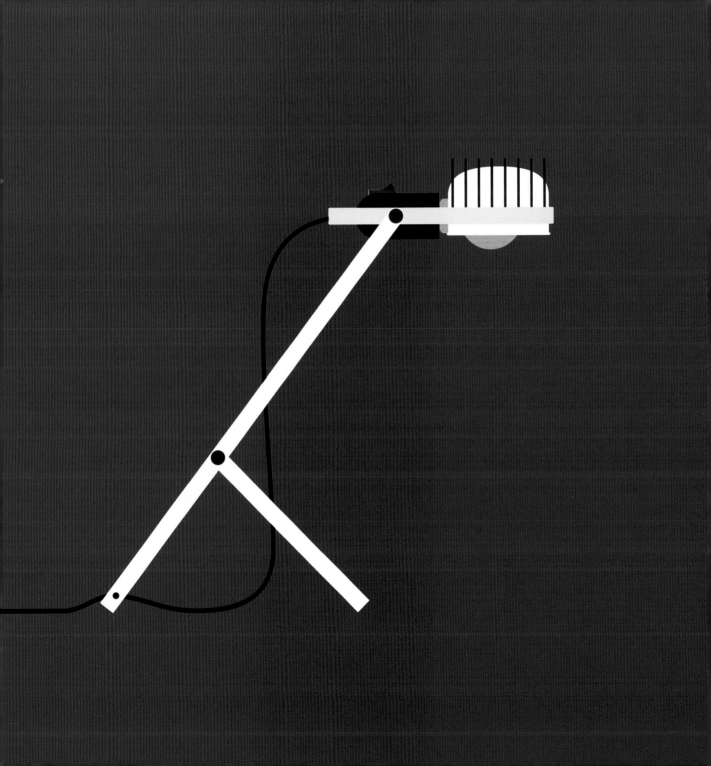

You like music. Why should you be bothered with technical complexity? With eight buttons on the remote to control volume or choose your music station (or record player), here is a simple interface between user and product. It makes the life of audio aficionados easier without compromising quality. The two Danish engineers who founded the company understood there are consumers who love music but not electronics. They perfected how you interact with the device, hiding functions less used under a panel next to the touch buttons on the receiver.

BANG + OLUFSEN
Beomaster 2400
Denmark 1976
Jacob Jensen (Danish)

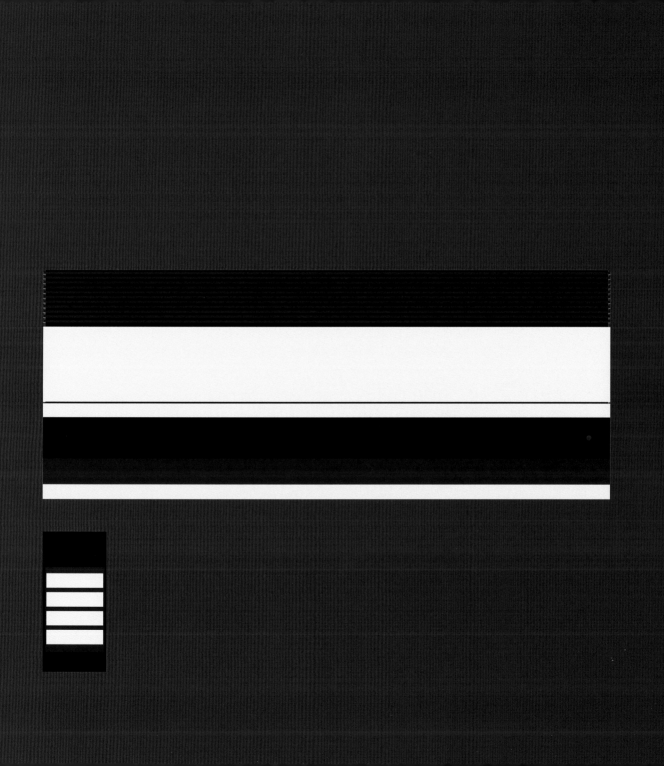

Some like it hot. And to keep your liquids that way, this product does the job, thanks to an ingenious lid. It pivots to let the steaming coffee out when you incline the carafe to pour but swings back to close when you set it down. All that, thanks to gravity and smart design. And that little black dot on the side? It's the visible part of the inner mechanism that holds it in place. It also indicates the pivoting point of the lid, for visual feedback.

STELTON
Thermal Carafe
Denmark 1976
Erik Magnusson (Danish)

Let there be light. But also here. And
there. This designer created a lamp that
shines down, provides diffuse light around
the center, and ever-so-slightly reflects
some of the light upward. With admirable
simplicity, he just added a suspended
disk with a hole. Illuminating us in more
than one way, this lamp is testimony to the
talent of its creator.

FLOS
Frisbi
Italy 1978
Achille Castiglioni (Italian)

A message in a bottle. It reads: perfect for an active lifestyle. Optimum choice of materials—hygienic plastic for the mouthpiece, reliable silicone rubber for the seals, and lightweight aluminum to reduce the weight—makes it ideal for energetic activities. Right down to the detail that lets you open it with your mouth while on the run.

This product has its priorities straight. The revolutionary idea behind this receiver/amplifier/ tape recorder/record player combination lies in the rigidity of the layout. Buttons, dials, and switches have been laid out in a grid. Vertical separation divides functions assigned to each component from left to right. Horizontal areas are arranged according to the frequency of their use. Main buttons are placed closest to the user, readouts being farthest away. This helps audiophiles who want all options at their fingertips but without confusion.

WEGA
Concept 51 K
Germany 1978
frogdesign, Hartmut Esslinger (German)

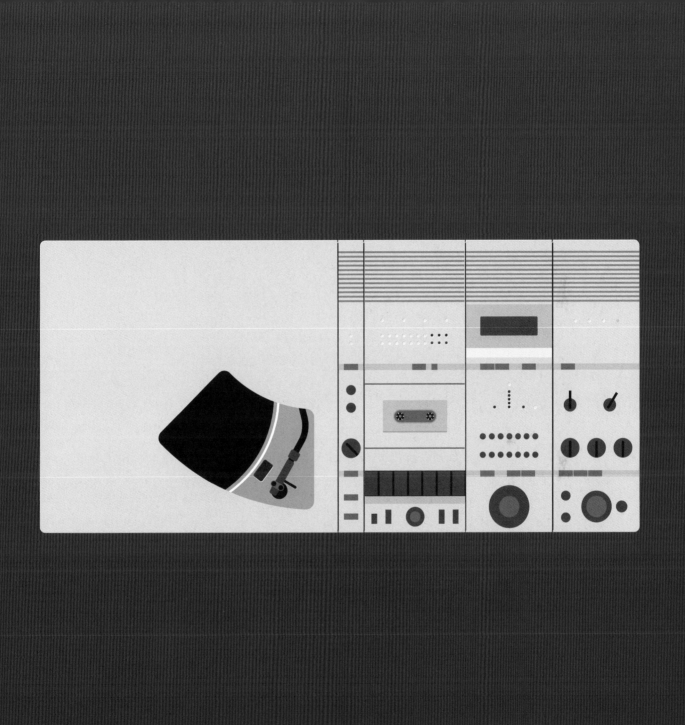

Come rain or come shine, with these shades you are prepared. You can swing up the nose bridge and exchange lenses to adapt to various light conditions. Using aviator sunglasses developed for the US Air Force in 1936 as a model, this design company created a modern version with replaceable lenses. They wrap comfortably around the head and protect against glare but also disguise a good part of the face if you want to go incognito.

CARRERA
Sunglasses
Austria 1979
Porsche Design (Austrian)

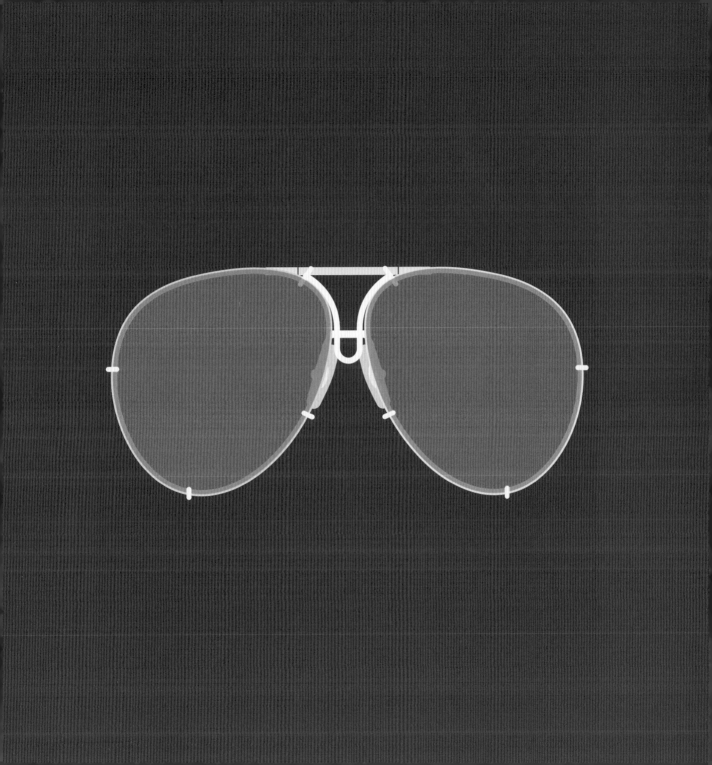

Afraid of the dark? Whether you are or you need your flashlight only for emergencies, you want to be able to rely on it. This outstanding lamp is rugged, easy to use, ergonomic, and reliable. Made of high-grade anodized aluminum, it features a krypton or xenon light source for the adjustable beam. The product has brought solid comfort to security forces and private citizens alike.

MAGLITE
Flashlight
United States of America 1979
Anthony Maglica (American)

It's a relief to find a public toilet when you need one. This is a hygienic space to answer the call of Nature—an intricate, free-standing container that cleans itself after each use. The looks are rugged, neutral, but sufficiently textured to discourage vandals, reassure citizens, and blend into any urban environment.

JCDECAUX
Public Toilet "Spea"
France 1980
Jean-Claude Decaux (French)

A tape recorder that does not record? The marketing department originally resisted. No wonder it took years before the idea— to wire a hifi amplifier to a simple cassette tape mechanism—took hold. Yet this little device changed our lives by enabling us to listen to music in high fidelity on the go. And for a while, it imbued the brand with a youthful spirit.

SONY
Walkman
Japan 1981
Sony Design Center (Japanese)

Get a grip. This razor invites you to hold
on tight with soft rubber dots protruding
its stainless-steel shell. Not only do the
dots give it a unique character, but they
also stand for the patented shearing foil
system of the shaving head. Innovative
in technology and design, this product
established the standard for shaving devices
and for product quality in general.

BRAUN
Micron Plus
Germany 1981
Roland Ullmann (German)

Life is an adventure. This versatile tool lets you deal with unexpected incidents. Inspired by pocket knives, the creator expanded on the idea by adding pliers. The quality of build, precision, and material choice of this versatile tool make it exceedingly popular. Surprisingly, this company is named not after the sturdy leather pouches its tools come in, but after one of the founders.

LEATHERMAN
Pocket Survival Tool
United States of America 1982
Timothy S. Leatherman (American)

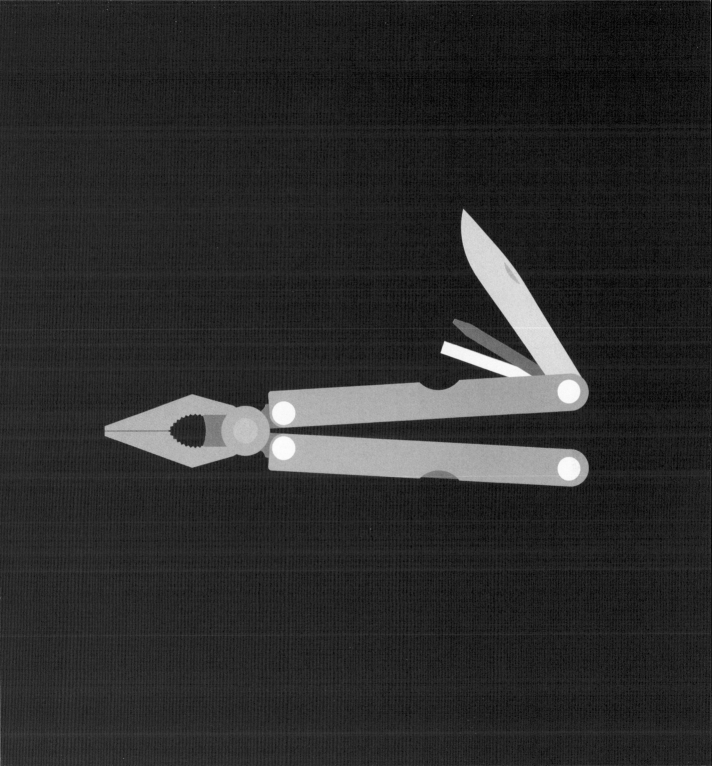

You can see right through it because it's plastic. When some Swiss members of the watch industry developed the idea of a plastic analog watch, they turned the market in their favor. With heavy investment in injection molding and ultrasonic welding, and using half the pieces of a comparable watch, they managed not only to reduce the production price to a fraction, but also to offer high-precision watches in a range of styles. Although this model was not the company's first, it most beautifully displayed the new plastic technology by its transparency, something classic watches could not do.

SWATCH
Jelly Fish
Switzerland 1983
unknown

You want to hear when the water is ready for your beverage. Here, a triple pipe announces the boiling point harmoniously. With a steel body and a plastic handle to protect from the heat, this kettle is a visual statement. In the mid-eighties, an array of designer kettles suddenly appeared on the market. Very few were as clever as this one.

ALESSI
Bollitore
Italy 1984
Richard Sapper (German)

A little friend on your desktop. The company founder himself insisted on a screen closer to the front, as he did not like the screen's frame looking like "furrowed brows" hanging over it. The device's frontal appearance, deliberately proportionally different from other personal computers, showed its innovation level. From its graphic user interface to the mouse, it heralded industry firsts. It's hard to understand how paradigm-shifting this design was, but it was indeed revolutionary.

APPLE
Macintosh
United States of America 1984
Steve Jobs, Jerry Manock, Terry Oyama (all American)

How did people communicate before mobile telephones? Today, we can hardly imagine what life was like without this brilliant technical innovation. When this company produced the first commercially available mobile phone that deserved the name, it was the beginning of an era. The design emphasized that everything—battery, antenna, receiver, and all the works—was self-contained. Though a little bulky by today's standards, it was compact.

MOTOROLA
Dyna Tac 8000 X
United States of America 1984
unknown

Who likes to be awakened by an alarm? Nobody. At least this novel idea made the process of getting up easier. All you had to do was shout "Stop!" when it rang, and it went quiet. No fishing for the clock, no leaving the warm pillows. This provided a new comfort level and quality of interaction. The trademark clarity of the dial, the fine details, and the practical protective cover made it a perfect travel accessory, since it was small enough to pack, but big enough not to get lost.

BRAUN
AB 312 vsl
Germany 1985
Dietrich Lubs (German)

No heavy metal, all lightweight aluminum.
Polished profiles hide the spring mechanism.
The lampshade and the bulb fitting are finished
in matte aluminum. Restriction to one material,
subtle variation in surface treatment, simple lines
combined with excellent functionality. That's all
one needs in a lamp.

ARTEMIDE
Tolomeo
Italy 1986
Michele de Lucchi, Giancarlo Fassina (both Italian)

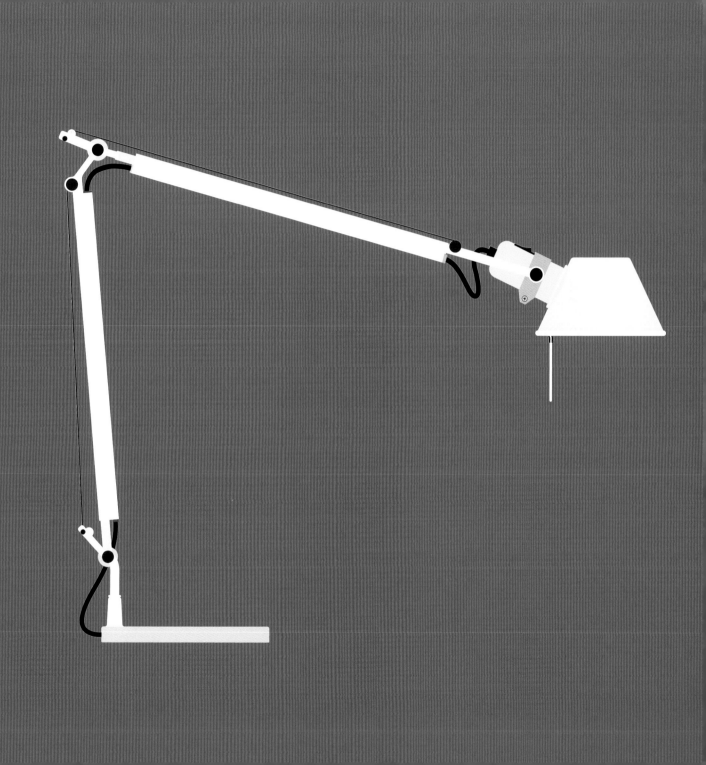

This is the real thing. You have probably seen
this design on your smartphone screen because
it inspired interface specialists generations later.
They adapted its design and layout for virtual
calculator keyboards on computers and mobile
devices. For the original, the designers, after
numerous experiments, determined concave
buttons were best for a keyboard like this. The
systematic application of subtle colors and the fine
detailing of the housing were masterful.

BRAUN
ET 66
Germany 1987
Dietrich Lubs, Dieter Rams (both German)

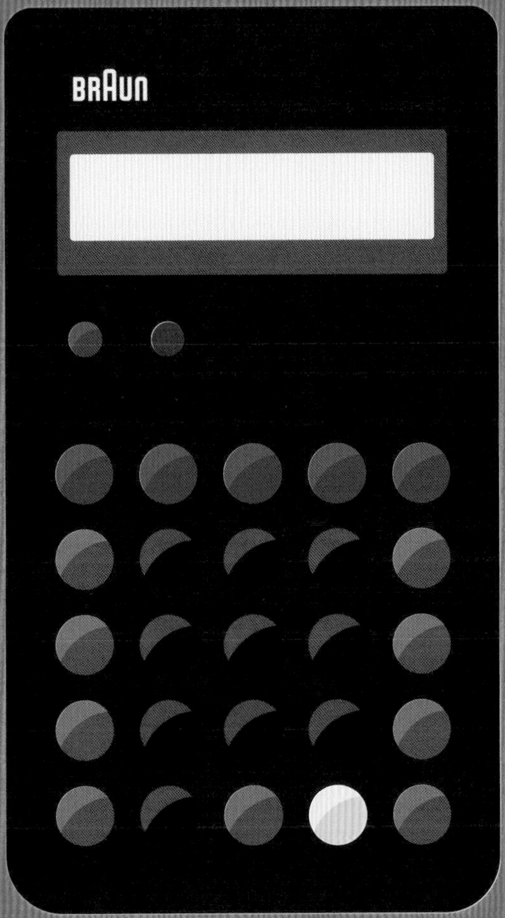
BRAUN

Take note. If you want it to be permanent, you had better use this marker. Graffiti artists, restaurant owners, company managers, teachers, scientists, and children have all chosen this pen for their distinct needs. Its popularity is testament not only to the quality of its tip and ink, but also to its size, proportion, and cap. Using empirical research, the designers developed the most ergonomic and easiest way to uncap it by creating little ribs, which also prevented the cap from rolling off the surface.

EDDING
Marker 3000
Germany 1987
Jens Plewa (German)

Light is more than waves and rays. For more than a hundred years, straight cones were used to indicate the physicality of light, which is a logical idea. This designer went metaphysical. He chose a cornucopia as a metaphor for the richness that light brings into our lives. Tipping the horn, which swivels on the pole, cleverly switches the light on and off.

FLOS
Ara Lamp
Italy 1988
Philippe Starck (French)

Not all of us live in a yellow submarine, but who wouldn't want to? Whether this tape player reminds you of maritime warning colors or of underwater vehicles from pop songs, its bold design, functional water protection cover, and rubberized buttons invite you to bring it along on the boat or to the beach. Most likely only a few of these were immersed in water, but the suggestive design hinted that you could if you just wanted to.

SONY
Walkman Sports
Japan 1988
Sony Design Center (Japanese)

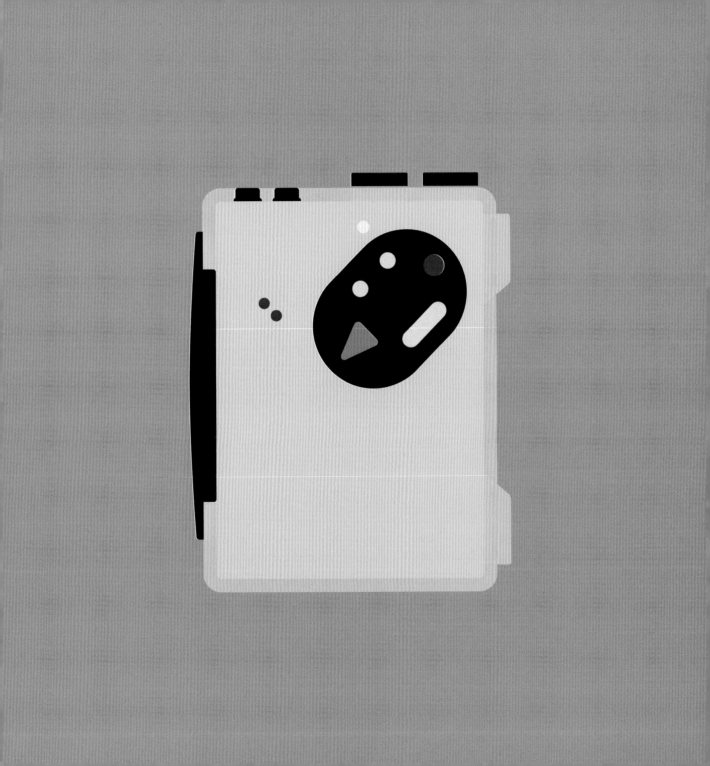

Does form follow function? And if so, which function? An excellent example of functionality's various meanings, this product made its designer famous and its manufacturer rich. In addition to its juicer function, it could serve as a very decorative present. In other words, it worked well on several levels. It almost seems too much to ask it to separate the seeds from the juice, which it doesn't.

ALESSI
Juicy Salif
Italy 1990
Philippe Starck (French)

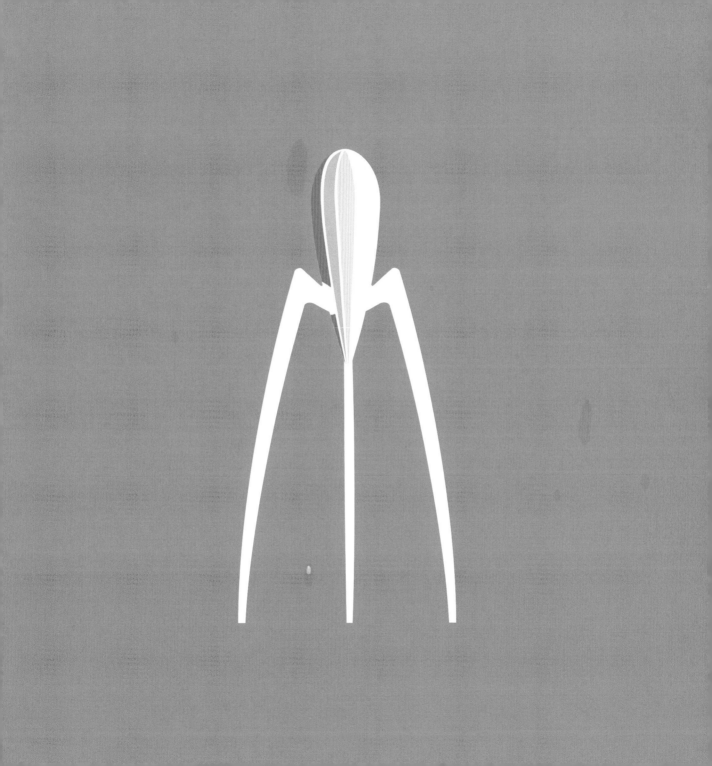

Regular vacuum cleaners collect dirt in bags. This outstandingly talented designer and engineer was unhappy with their effectiveness once those bags started to fill up. He applied his considerable engineering skills to improving how they work. Replacing the costly bag, which clogs up, he used a canister in which the impelled air rotates. The centrifugal forces separate the lighter air from the heavier dust. Emptying the canister is all the user has to do. The bold color scheme and expressive geometric shapes—never before seen on a household appliance of this size—effectively communicated the innovation.

DYSON
DC 01
United Kingdom 1993
James Dyson (English)

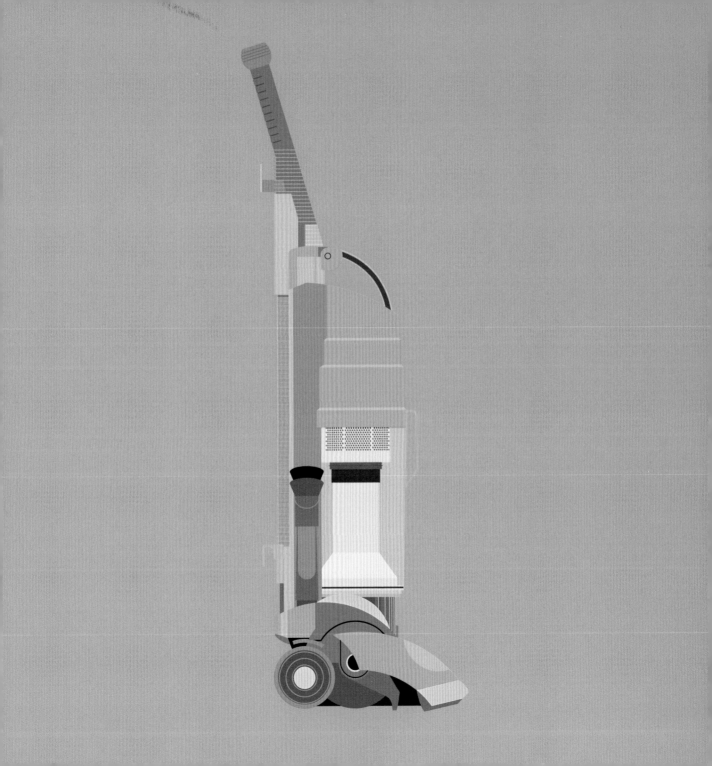

Designing for the elderly benefits us all.
Not only because we all hope to get older,
but because better ergonomics are always
an advantage. This smart design uses
soft silicone to provide a nonslip grip and
a comfortable place for the thumb while
peeling, making us all feel better about
this mundane task. Planned for a small
market segment, it enjoyed surprisingly
broad success. The principle has since been
applied to a wide range of kitchen gadgets.

OXO
Peeler
United States of America 1990
Smart Design (American)

Should products have personalities? Absolutely. Should they look like little people or creatures? Why not? This product was among the first of many gadgets where the function and its expression were not enough—at least in the eyes of the creator and the manufacturer. Whether that is appropriate depends on if you see this primarily as a bottle opener or, more important, as a fun accessory to celebrate happy times. The name of the product and the hairstyle of the character are references to a colleague and friend of the designer, Anna Gili.

ALESSI
Anna G.
Italy 1994
Alessandro Mendini (Italian)

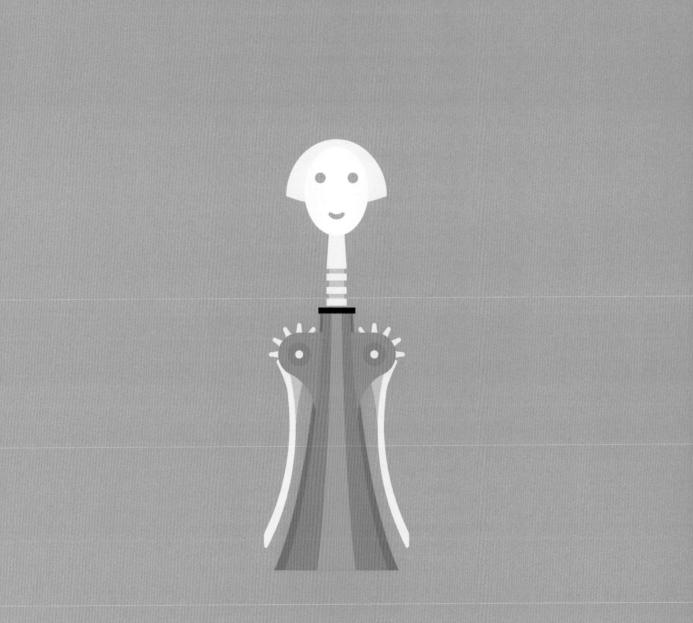

A fun computer. Why? Because computers could be more than tools for the office; they could also provide entertainment. After the Macintosh was established as a truly personal computer for the home and work, the Internet arrived, and with it all the fun websites, online gaming, and access to information. To acknowledge our increasing use of computers for pastime pleasures, this company dared to be bold. Transparent housing in a range of lively colors let us peek inside. It was not just a pretty face, since it could provide the performance necessary to fulfill any task. It was also the company's first product with an 'i,' denoting its easy Internet access, but also referring to individual, imagination, and innovation.

APPLE
iMac
United States of America 1998
Jony Ive (English)

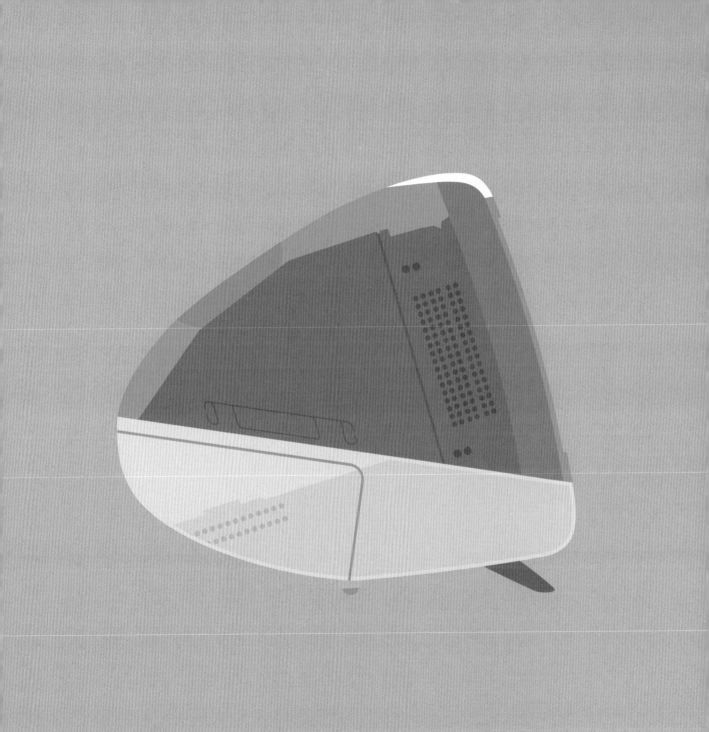

A bike with smaller tires needs an improved suspension. This brilliant engineer invented a rubber cone suspension system for his friend Alec Issigonis's minicar. Then he developed several bicycles that also featured rubber suspension and small wheels. Improving the frame, he extended it sideways and labelled it Spaceframe. The resulting construction was compact, but lightweight and stiff and looked different. It had an architectural quality.

MOULTON
Spaceframe Bicycle
United Kingdom 1998
Alex Moulton (English)

We want information at our fingertips, or in the palm of our hands. Preceding smartphones, personal digital assistants (PDAs) like this one paved the way for mobile electronic organizers. A must-have for professionals, they contained calendars, address files, and messages. Among the many models, this one stood out due to its technical specifications. The metal housing included an integrated rechargeable battery. The anodized aluminum shell looked sleek and was more scratch-proof than previous plastic models.

3M
Palm V
United States of America 1999
IDEO (American)

You have to pull some strings to get this player working. An amazing idea—no buttons on this exemplary minimalistic CD player, just a loudspeaker. Simply pull the power cord; the motor spins and the disk plays until the cord is pulled again. This designer knew exactly how to make a music device fun, whimsical, and intuitive. The loudspeaker pattern gave it enough visual interest to be familiar, yet not boring.

MUJI
CD Player
Japan 1999
Naoto Fukasawa (Japanese)

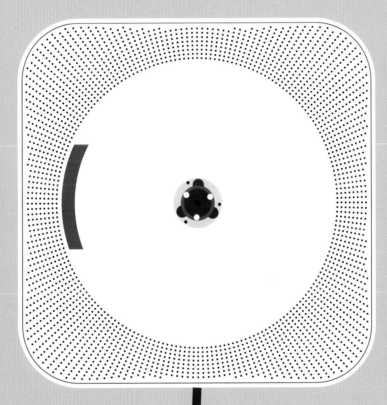

Immortal—mobile phones from this company had a reputation for being indestructible. The unique exchangeable shells meant you could replace them when they got scratched, and you could customize. A range of colors and surfaces was available. In spite of the double walls that the shells created, it was also quite slim and easy to handle.

NOKIA
8210
Finland 1999
unknown

Meant for a quiet day at home. The first desktop computer without a ventilator, it featured a silver metal cube floating in a plexiglass "cage." CDs ejected vertically in a rather theatrical way. Using a touch-button main switch just added to the feeling of effortlessly efficient electronics at your fingertips, perfect for home, office, and private use alike.

APPLE
Cube
United States of America 2000
Apple Design Team (American)

Carry all your songs in your pocket. This small package could hold days of music. With the company's newly created music software, the way we consume music was turned upside down. Easy and fast download of songs from the largest record companies for a standard fee, combined with the ability to arrange titles into "playlists" and listen on the go —that was revolutionary. The inspiration for the design clearly came from Braun's earlier radio models, as the designer freely conceded. Obviously, he shared the idea that nothing should distract from the experience.

APPLE
iPod
United States of America 2000
Jony Ive (English)

Comfortable as a throne for a king, reminiscent of centuries-old shapes. Few designers can pull that off in transparent, injection-molded plastic. Improving the ergonomics of the era pieces by creating a very pleasant seat and adding stack-ability are proof of the designer's mastery. Who would think plastic could be so comfortable? When asked, he responded: "I don't like to sit on a corpse"—dramatically exaggerating his turning away from designing chairs upholstered with leather.

KARTELL
Louis Ghost
Italy 2002
Philippe Starck (French)

Humans are mobile and smart. Why shouldn't their phones be, too? When this computer company entered the mobile phone market, people queued up to snatch one of the first samples. The aura and reputation of the company accrued to its unknown product. Today, after several iterations, the phone itself has achieved iconic status, thanks to its quality, versatility, and uncompromising minimalism. Rather than designing an object that draws attention to itself, the goal was obviously to create a perfect frame, an ideal canvas for all types of content appearing on it.

APPLE
iPhone
United States of America 2007
Apple Design Team (American)

The second mouse gets the cheese. This one gets admiration for its perfection. When the inventor Douglas Engelbart came forward with his idea for a pointing device, he could not have guessed its roaring success. After mechanical capture, laser optics now do the job. Buttons have been replaced by a surface that pivots for clicking and serves as a touch pad at the same time. The surface is smooth with extraordinarily improved functionality. Amazing construction quality, with a metal injection-molded bottom and battery cover, completes this magical device.

APPLE
Magic Mouse
United States of America 2009
Apple Design Team (American)

In the eye of the storm, the air is calm. This fan—labeled "air multiplier" to underline its innovative technology—features a big hole where normally the blades would be. Few companies are pursuing innovation with such fervor. From the more powerful, yet more silent motor to the original airflow, every detail has been reconsidered and improved to blow all similar products away. The result is a new and spectacular object. Its design has a sculptural quality and visual impact that is not only on a par with the technology, but strongly communicates it.

DYSON
Air Multiplier
United Kingdom 2009
James Dyson (English)

Photo: Juan Yuste, Madrid/London

About the Author

For more than a quarter century, I have worked as a designer with start-ups like Hommage to multinational giants like Samsung, and on products ranging from rubber ducks to gas chromatographs. My creative credo? To make products easier to use and understand by designing them expressively. And, though beauty is a subjective concept, I care about it deeply. While I always hope my designs will become iconic, the closest I've come so far is having a coffee machine, which I designed for Switzerland's most valuable brand, JURA, in the largest German design museum in Munich.

I started my design career working with Pentagram in London and frogdesign in the Black Forest. In 1988, I opened my own design office, now VIEWSDESIGN, located in the Saint-Germain-des-Prés area of Paris, where I work on product, interface, and brand design. My friend and partner Lutz Gebhardt runs VIEWSDESIGN Switzerland in Basel.

Simultaneous to my design work, I became an educator at age thirty-one when I was appointed chairman for product design at Art Center College of Design, on its European campus in Switzerland. After that, I was named Directeur des Diplômes at Strate College in Paris. During the same period, I became professor and department chair at a new Swiss design school, planning and running its product design department. I also taught design management at universities in Solothurn and Zürich, and at the International Management Institute in Lausanne.

Being a teacher is a mind-set, not an occupation, as much as a school is not a house, but individuals sharing knowledge. Design has to explain and to inspire, and in my two decades of working in education, I have done the same, trying to enlighten and to stimulate young talents.

Through my engineer father and my arts and crafts teacher mother, I was exposed to scientific and artistic influence. As I was born in South Africa and have resided in Germany, the United Kingdom, Switzerland, South Korea, and California before moving to Paris, France gave me a broad cultural perspective. Picking up languages along the way, I discovered parallels between linguistic and design thinking. Shapes, details, and colors are vocabulary, and designing with these elements requires syntax and grammar, and this is how I communicate, by addressing emotions as well as the rational mind.

As much as design does and should speak for itself, there is information, background, and context that I feel worth sharing with people, which is why I decided to write this book.

List of Designers

List of Manufacturers

Bibliography / Sources

For this book, I have researched in books and online. The books I have used are listed below, without indication as to which page has provided information about which product.

Schnellkurs Design, Dumont 1995, Thomas Hauffe, ISBN 3-7701-3388-9

Le Design Book, Phaidon 2013, ISBN 978-0-7148-6696-6

Design heute, Prestel 1988, Volker Fischer, ISBN 3-7913-0854-8

Iconic Designs, Bloomsbury 2014, Grace Lees-Maffei, ISBN 9780-8578-5352-3

The Design Encyclopedia, The Museum of Modern Art 1994, 2004, Mel Byars, ISBN 0 87070 012 x

Researching online, I have used Wikipedia mainly for verification and will not list those articles here; also no websites from companies that produce or have in the past produced the respective product. Other websites with information pertaining to specific products are listed below, in chronological order of the product launch, as sorted in this book.

THONET • No.14 • Thonet Brothers

Le Design Book, Phaidon, p 018, ISBN 978 0 7148 6696 6

http://bit.ly/2BiOo1T
http://bit.ly/2rpFVdj
http://bit.ly/2DWMmr4

HOPE GLASS WORKS • Mineral Water Bottle • Hiram Codd

http://bit.ly/2Bjj7LY
http://bit.ly/2DWH3aW
http://bit.ly/2mZgt9X
http://bit.ly/2DwW9XN

DIMPLE • Whisky Bottle • unknown

http://bit.ly/2mWlDmd
http://bit.ly/2DnCMwe
http://bit.ly/2DuXSw7

VICTORINOX • Pocket Knife • Wester&Co

http://bit.ly/2ghjX66
http://bit.ly/2BjFYXT
http://bit.ly/2G1f5vy

OPINEL • No.10 Knife • Joseph Opinel

http://bit.ly/2F2Mvs7
http://bit.ly/2DviGED
http://bit.ly/2DUKY8c

MASON PEARSON • Hairbrush • Mason Pearson

http://bit.ly/2mYMQor

http://bit.ly/2EZXZg6

http://bit.ly/ZpWeoo

COCA-COLA • Coke Bottle • Earl R.Dean

http://read.bi/2rufhQN

http://bit.ly/2qpeUBc

http://bit.ly/2DyabYh

KITCHEN AID • Mixer • Herbert Johnson

http://bit.ly/2F1AdjU

http://bit.ly/2mYQL4z

http://bit.ly/2Bk9Aoa

UNKNOWN • Red Telephone Box • Giles Gilbert Scott

http://bit.ly/2noNz9p

http://bit.ly/1n1986K

http://bit.ly/2BiqyDc

./. • Lamp • Wilhelm Wagenfeld

http://bit.ly/2DYoPCU

http://bit.ly/2rqen7E

http://bit.ly/2DAKfLE

LE CREUSET • French Oven • Octave Aubecq, Armand Desaegher

http://bit.ly/2mZ8UjL

https://ind.pn/2Bjkg6e

http://bit.ly/2DyaiTH

THONET • Cantilever Chair • Marcel Breuer

http://nyti.ms/1vXJApV

http://bit.ly/2mZAMUL

http://bit.ly/2mZ9vB8

./. • Iron • Walter Dorwin Teague

http://bit.ly/2mtaN5i

http://bit.ly/2Dp3Prd

http://bit.ly/2noFK3P

SCHOTT • Tea Pot • Wilhelm Wagenfeld

http://bit.ly/2Bh9KwF

http://bit.ly/2Du8QCF

http://bit.ly/2DYdqX2

./. • Anglepoise Lamp • George Carwardine

http://bit.ly/2EYCTyU

http://bit.ly/2DuRzJP

http://bit.ly/1BQ6YXy

DR.G.SEIBT • VW301W • Walter Maria Kersting

http://bit.ly/2DnqHHf

http://bit.ly/2lEbnOJ

http://bit.ly/2mwZXv6

ZIPPO • lighter • George G.Blaisdell

http://bit.ly/2DqORB2

http://bit.ly/2DmQSOr

http://bit.ly/2DvTjCE

HOMER LAUGHLIN CHINA CO. • Fiestaware • Frederick Hurten Rhead

http://bit.ly/2rrvm9R
http://bit.ly/2mWfjfx
http://bit.ly/2FZVlIH

WESTERN ELECTRIC • 302 • Phone • Henry Dreyfuss

http://bit.ly/1PdHsco
http://bit.ly/2DAKCpw
http://bit.ly/2G3JuJJ

KODAK • Bantam Special • Walter Dorwin Teague

http://bit.ly/2BjUFKw
http://bit.ly/2GoATaJ
http://bit.ly/2DnhIWS

MINOX • Riga Camera • Walter Zapp

http://bit.ly/2DvJHrt
http://bit.ly/2mXrsjD
http://bit.ly/2FZVGLt

RIMOWA • Aluminum Luggage • Richard Morszek

http://bit.ly/2EYDhNS
http://bit.ly/2DwExum
http://bit.ly/2DmdKop

SWANN-MORTON • Scalpel • unknown

http://bit.ly/2BizqZN
http://bit.ly/2G3lMNp

BIALETTI • Moka Express • Alfonso Bialetti

http://bit.ly/1OZCtt1
https://ind.pn/2DoR5AI
http://cnn.it/1UbYB63

S.T.DUPONT • Lighter • unknown

http://bit.ly/2mYXNXQ
http://bit.ly/2mWMoYo
http://bit.ly/2BhWIib

KODAK • Brownie Six-20 • unknown

http://bit.ly/1NxrQuM
http://bit.ly/1zAtuIF
http://www.brownie.camera

HOWARD MILLER • Ball Clock • George Nelson

http://bit.ly/2DX2nNQ
http://bit.ly/2mZ7Pby
http://bit.ly/2mYKANR

MOVADO • Museum Watch • Nathan Gordon Levitt

http://bit.ly/2Du1bEz
http://bit.ly/2DpenGB
http://bit.ly/2DWYRTF

BUSH • TV 22 • unknown

http://bbc.in/2GoBZmR
http://bit.ly/2mYOfv8
http://bit.ly/2DWIu9z

CITROËN • 2CV • Flaminio Bertoni

http://bit.ly/2DzD9qI

http://bit.ly/2rmRYYW

http://bit.ly/2mYOiqO

BIC • Cristal Pen • Décolletage Plastique

http://bit.ly/2GoC6yN

http://bit.ly/1ulHVYO

http://bit.ly/2EZ7DQo

PAVONI • Europiccola • unknown

http://bit.ly/2EZ7VX6

http://bit.ly/2DwE8YP

http://bit.ly/2EYEgO4

WEBER • Grill • George A. Stephen

http://bit.ly/2Dr8U6a

http://s.si.edu/1q3IkIC

http://bit.ly/2kKX77V

BAUSCH & LOMB • Ray Ban Wayfarer • Raymond Stegeman

http://bit.ly/2Bj5TyQ

http://bit.ly/2DwwEoW

http://bit.ly/2Dp2GzM

ESGE • Zauberstab • Acton Bjørn

http://bit.ly/2n2AKbS

http://bit.ly/2G2bbSU

http://bit.ly/2DvT7TS

FENDER • Stratocaster • Leo Fender, Bill Carson, George Fullerton, Freddie Tavares

http://bit.ly/2DUDu5h

http://bit.ly/2bH5RtZ

http://bit.ly/2GoEqWx

LONDON TRANSPORT • Routemaster • A.A.M. Durant, Douglas Scott

http://bit.ly/2F2byM9

http://bit.ly/2Dv2keS

http://bit.ly/2mWh1xt

ROSTI • Margrethe Bowl • Sigvard Bernadotte, Acton Bjørn

http://bit.ly/2DW9GFs

http://bit.ly/2mWpKyF

http://bit.ly/2mYXNHu

PIAGGIO • Vespa • Corradino d'Ascanio

http://bit.ly/2Du1Dmf

http://bit.ly/2BhTY4z

http://bit.ly/2BirHLo

BRAUN • SK4 • Hans Gugelot, Dieter Rams

http://bit.ly/2mZqzYl

http://bit.ly/2G3n6jl

http://bit.ly/R98AN2

BRAUN • T3 • Dieter Rams

http://bit.ly/2Dpf4zH

http://on.ft.com/2G3nJJJ
http://bit.ly/2F1ivNF

LOUIS POULSEN • Artichoke Lamp • Poul Henningsen
https://ind.pn/23W8wB0
http://bit.ly/1O2nF8j
http://bit.ly/1V2KNcs

ROLODEX • Address File • Hildaur Neilsen
http://bit.ly/2DwFDXo
http://bit.ly/2DsYqmS
http://bit.ly/2DBocl2

MONO • A • Peter Raacke
http://bit.ly/2G2MsOi
http://bit.ly/2DtvdIn
http://bit.ly/2n3bo2b

SONY • 8-301 • unknown
http://bit.ly/2kuR84F
http://bit.ly/2GoA4yv
http://bit.ly/2DzSWpO

THOMAS • TC 100 • Nick Roehricht
http://bit.ly/2rtHhE2
http://bit.ly/2DBohFm
http://ubm.io/2mYP7jo

BULOVA • Accutron • unknown
http://bit.ly/2mZcx8u
http://bit.ly/2DULzqr
http://bit.ly/2DWKMVY

FLOS • Arco • Achille & Pier Castiglioni
http://bit.ly/2FoP2ml
http://bit.ly/2DkDSJ5
https://ind.pn/2EYFTLG

OHIO ART COMPANY • Etch A Sketch • André Cassagnes
http://bit.ly/1TqLvjt
http://bit.ly/2mWrRT7
http://ti.me/2DwxSk2

VITRA • Chair • Verner Panton
http://bit.ly/2DuZypp
https://ind.pn/1yJGgAI
http://bit.ly/2DxQm4o

IBM • Selectric • Eliot Noyes
http://bit.ly/2DAoBnQ
http://engt.co/2DWEozB
http://bit.ly/2DUzsd4

KIKKOMAN • Soy Sauce Bottle • Kenji Ekuan
http://bit.ly/2DtbYil
http://mo.ma/2EZK2Pf
http://nyti.ms/2mYZ9C4

BRAUN • MX 32 • Gerd Alfred Müller, Robert Oberheim
http://bit.ly/2DvVAOc

BRAUN • Sixtant SM 31 • Gugelot, Müller
http://bit.ly/2G1tp7f
http://bit.ly/2BisZ8O
hhttp://bit.ly/2DV1TYv

HAVAIANAS • Flip-flop sandals • Robert Fraser
http://bit.ly/2DVSFv2
http://bit.ly/2BieovE
http://on.ft.com/2rntLCo

VIEW-MASTER • Model G • unknown
http://bit.ly/2BiYXBY
http://bit.ly/2rwUoob
http://bit.ly/1RnUDm6

BRIONVEGA • Cubo • Richard Sapper, Marco Zanuso
http://bit.ly/2BhYVtZ
http://bit.ly/1npiGaE
http://bit.ly/2Du5gIP

KODAK • Carousel • Hans Gugelot, Reinhold Hacker
http://nyti.ms/2noPN8L
http://bit.ly/2Dtw1Np
http://bit.ly/2DvUT7u

PENTEL • Sign Pen (Fiber Tip Pen) • Yukio Horie
http://bit.ly/2BgQBut

http://bit.ly/2BjNL7Z
http://bit.ly/2rtI8Vg

BRIONVEGA • Algol • Richard Sapper, Marco Zanuso
http://bit.ly/2mZznoG
http://bit.ly/2DpTsn3
http://bit.ly/2mYEDBC

OLIVETTI • Programma 101 • Mario Bellini
http://bit.ly/1sRr8DQ
http://bit.ly/2rwWo1d
http://bit.ly/2Bju3ct

O-LUCE • Spider • Joe Colombo
http://bit.ly/2F2dlRn
http://bit.ly/2mYOQwP

STUDIO M • Bulb • Ingo Maurer
http://bit.ly/2DxSaKl
http://mo.ma/2DrhA8s
http://bit.ly/2DAOA1o

FISKARS • O-Series • Olof Bäckström
http://bit.ly/2DWfE9k
http://bit.ly/2ru2D3Y
http://bit.ly/2mXAFsd

GDB • Mineral Water Bottle • Günter Kupetz
http://bit.ly/2mWvvMN
http://bit.ly/2DuTIFe
http://bit.ly/2DWOJtM

KODAK • Instamatic • Kenneth Grange

http://bit.ly/2o8XpEh

http://bit.ly/2DzLwCU

http://bit.ly/2FoP1zm

VLM • Light Switch • Achille Castiglioni

http://bit.ly/2DxXaPe

http://bit.ly/2DlB2Uh

OLIVETTI • Valentine • Ettore Sottsass

http://bit.ly/2G2HL7w

http://bit.ly/2mYaMJg

http://bit.ly/2p9d8qm

ROSENTHAL • Tea Pot • Walter Gropius

http://bit.ly/2BiCxAX

http://bit.ly/2DlB5PX

http://bit.ly/2mX4SHH

BRAUN • HLD 4 • Dieter Rams

http://bit.ly/2DV5mpZ

http://bit.ly/2mWj98r

http://bit.ly/2G1dzte

ARTEMIDE • Tizio • Richard Sapper

http://bit.ly/2G1dHJe

http://mo.ma/2EZlBRo

http://bit.ly/2DUJWsY

CINI & NILS • Cuboluce • Franco Bettonica, Mario Melocchi

http://bit.ly/2DuVSEZ

http://bit.ly/2F35fb7

http://bit.ly/2EZIwga

DENNERT & PAPE • Aristo M65 • unknown

http://bit.ly/2no5oFy

http://bit.ly/2BjuNyh

http://bit.ly/2FoSJsA

FLOS • Parentesi • Pio Manzù, Achille Castiglioni

http://bit.ly/2G3rcrJ

http://bit.ly/2F1swua

http://bit.ly/2DwHiMb

OLIVETTI • Divisumma 18 • Mario Bellini

http://bit.ly/2EZdu7W

http://bit.ly/2mZoLLV

http://bit.ly/2mXl8JA

POLAROID • SX-70 • Henry Dreyfuss

http://bit.ly/2DWVonY

http://bit.ly/2Dv23bh

http://bit.ly/2G1qBH5

WEGA • TV 3050 • Esslinger Design

http://bit.ly/2DnoM5K

http://bit.ly/2mWln6Q

BIC • lighter • Louis Lucien Lepoix

http://bit.ly/2Dv6nb4

http://bit.ly/2BgT9sx

LIP • Dark Master • Roger Tallon

http://bit.ly/2DnHElo

http://bit.ly/2FoXNoc

http://bit.ly/2DqyAvN

SINCLAIR • Black Watch • Clive Sinclair

http://bit.ly/2FoXPoQ

http://bit.ly/2DvYna8

http://bit.ly/2mYRvHZ

ARTEMIDE • Sintesi • Ernesto Gismondi

http://bit.ly/2GojA9w

http://bit.ly/2EYllxh

BANG+OLUFSEN • Beomaster 2400 • Jacob Jensen

http://bit.ly/2Foytav

http://bit.ly/2rwXCbh

http://bit.ly/2no5EEw

STELTON • Thermal Carafe • Erik Magnusson

http://bit.ly/2mYXNHu

http://bit.ly/2G3S1MK

FLOS • Frisbi • Achille Castiglioni

http://bit.ly/2DomP9f

SIGG • Water Bottle • Kurt Zimmerli

http://bit.ly/2DUKoaE

http://bit.ly/2mWTXOa

WEGA • Concept 51 K • frogdesign Hartmut Esslinger

http://bit.ly/2DwAcYi

http://bit.ly/2rvrJQm

http://bit.ly/2DuMqAH

CARRERA • Sunglasses • Porsche Design

http://bit.ly/2DBfmqD

MAGLIGHT • Flashlight • Anthony Maglica

http://bit.ly/2FXTiVs

http://n.pr/2DWKFK7

http://nyp.st/1GBVZs6

JCDECAUX • SPEA • Jean-Claude Decaux

http://bit.ly/2mZtIY9

http://bit.ly/2G3Q6b1

SONY • Walkman • Sony Design Center

http://bit.ly/1ql43Eq

http://ti.me/1lx1HMK

http://bit.ly/1T6P2n1

BRAUN • Micron Plus • Roland Ullmann

http://bit.ly/2FoRzNW

http://bit.ly/2mXDCsN

http://bit.ly/2DpXETP

LEATHERMAN • Pocket Survival Tool • Timothe S. Leatherman
http://bit.ly/2Dtb858
http://bit.ly/2DubLLJ
http://tcrn.ch/2Drj9TS

SWATCH • Jelly Fish • unknown
http://tcrn.ch/2mWjYy3
http://bit.ly/2DBfTsD
http://bit.ly/2mZu7K9

ALESSI • Bollitore • Richard Sapper
http://bit.ly/TX5xbC

APPLE • Macintosh • Jobs, Mannock, Oyama
http://bit.ly/2DTqDQJ
http://bit.ly/2l9xvjB
http://bit.ly/1avfNQ4

MOTOROLA • Dyna Tac 8000 X • unknown
http://bit.ly/1FmwHfx
http://ti.me/TkQngH
http://bit.ly/2DvoIFh

BRAUN • AB 312 vsl • Dietrich Lubs
http://bit.ly/2mZc2fm

ARTEMIDE • Tolomeo • Michele de Lucchi, Giancarlo Fassina
http://bit.ly/2DUWosJ
http://bit.ly/2mWkgF9
http://bit.ly/2DxUtNS

BRAUN • ET66 • Dieter Rams, Dietrich Lubs
http://bit.ly/2G1AtRj
http://bit.ly/2DSwnKt
http://bit.ly/2DUMjMo

EDDING • Marker • Jens Plewa
http://bit.ly/2mYCXlm
http://bit.ly/2DYYojT
http://bit.ly/2DxPXoV

FLOS • Ara • Philippe Starck
http://bit.ly/2DowigK
http://bit.ly/2n12ouh
http://bit.ly/2G2Sf6u

SONY • Walkman Sports • Sony Design Center
http://bit.ly/1ql43Eq
http://bit.ly/2G1ch1f

ALESSI • Juicy Salif • Philippe Starck
https://ind.pn/2eRJfYq
http://bit.ly/2rpEBHF

OXO • Peeler • Smart Design
http://bit.ly/1jTDjlk
http://s.si.edu/2Dv8lZo
http://bit.ly/2FoTSAo

DYSON • DC 01 • James Dyson
http://bit.ly/2DvQrWj
http://on.inc.com/2jO53SL
http://bit.ly/2DUJhYz

ALESSI • Anna G • Alessandro Mendini

http://bit.ly/2DX8f9R

http://on.ft.com/2G2LxxI

http://bit.ly/2G3TgeS

APPLE • iMac • Jony Ive

http://apple-history.com/imac

http://bit.ly/2DUiHP8

http://bit.ly/1avfNQ4

http://bit.ly/2rp5Hyt

MOULTON • Spaceframe bicycle • unknown

http://bit.ly/2mZBUrl

http://bit.ly/2Du7bgz

http://bit.ly/2BiNEJZ

3M • Palm Pilot V • IDEO

http://bit.ly/2DV982D

http://bit.ly/2DomPWL

http://bit.ly/2mYWzer

http://bit.ly/2DnBXU8

MUJI • CD Player • Naoto Fukasawa

http://bit.ly/2DvZeYk

http://bit.ly/2Don7wP

http://bit.ly/2Bke9ii

NOKIA • 8210 • unknown

http://cnet.co/2DWilCm

http://bit.ly/2BiokRr

http://bit.ly/2BioqbL

APPLE • Cube • Apple Design Team

http://bit.ly/2GoMruB

http://engt.co/2pogTdh

http://bit.ly/2DpMFtg

APPLE • iPod • Jony Ive

http://bit.ly/1ECVjC1

http://cnet.co/2BkeaTo

http://apple-history.com/ipod

KARTELL • Louis Ghost • Philippe Starck

http://bit.ly/2DpiTEW

http://bit.ly/2Fosxyj

http://bit.ly/2Bjxfot

APPLE • iPhone • Apple Design Team

http://bit.ly/1vx2XJf

http://bit.ly/1TrEYGJ

http://bit.ly/1ROBhwl

APPLE • Magic Mouse • Apple Design Team

http://bit.ly/2DtgP33

http://bit.ly/2nom4Mi

DYSON • Air Multiplier • James Dyson

http://ti.me/2DUj2Bo

http://bit.ly/2mWovzC

http://bit.ly/15VBWWo